# Big Sky M

A Study of Montana's Macedonian-Americans

Victor Sinadinoski

*Macedonians of America Series*

Copyright © 2019 by Victor Sinadinoski
All rights reserved. This book or any portion thereof may not be reproduced or used in any manner whatsoever without the express written permission of the publisher except for the use of brief quotations.

Printed in the United States of America

ISBN: 978-1794471948

*For Montana's remaining Macedonians.*

*(This page intentionally left blank)*

# Introduction

When people speak about Macedonian immigration to the United States of America, Montana rarely enters the conversation. Usually, the discussion focuses on states that presently harbor visible Macedonian communities and Macedonian Orthodox churches, such as in Illinois, Indiana, Michigan, New Jersey, New York and Ohio. Historically, gainful employment and community resources were readily accessible to Macedonians in these states. The thriving Midwestern cities and metropolises provided manufacturing jobs, social services, and growing Balkan colonies during the early 20th century, which allowed for a smoother transition into American society. Today, Macedonian communities still flourish in these states and the available historical documentation of Macedonian immigration suggests that these states (except for New Jersey) have always been principal gathering points for Macedonian immigrants. Hence, the idea of Macedonians working and settling in Big Sky Country[1] is at best a distant memory: most Macedonians have no awareness of Macedonian immigration to Montana.

However, Macedonian immigration to Montana was a significant part of the Macedonian experience in the early 20th century and the evidence for this claim is plentiful. Still, there has been little exploration into the topic. The best-known description of the Macedonian immigrant experience in Montana comes from Stoyan Christowe, a Macedonian who immigrated to America in 1911 and proceeded to become a respected journalist, author and Vermont politician. He first settled in St. Louis, Missouri with an uncle before they, along with a large group of Macedonians, abandoned the city to work on the Great Northern Railway in Montana.

At first, Christowe hesitated to give up his job at a shoe factory for a water boy position in Montana. His uncle recognized that Christowe was too young and small for the intense physical labor involved in track building, but he still wanted his nephew to come with him. Plus, every railroad section gang needed a water boy. Christowe's uncle proceeded to persuade him:

**But you'll be making more in Montana. Thirteen cents an hour, ten hours a day. Sundays, too, and overtime. No rent to pay. Besides, there's grass and trees there, and mountains. That's what everybody says that's been there. Just think, you can see the water you drink come out of the earth, just like in the old country. Mitko says you can even get eggs from real hens. Just think!**[2]

Realizing he had little to risk, Christowe joined his uncle and about 100 other Macedonians in the journey to Montana.[3] (In his autobiography, *This Is My Country*, Christowe details his Montana experience for nearly 60 pages, describing in detail Macedonian life in the bunk cars and the intricacies of working on the railroad.)

    Macedonians immigrated westward to places like Montana for several reasons, as Christowe highlighted in his autobiography. The overarching reason, however, was that Montana had jobs that begged for cheap labor, especially during the first two decades of the 20th century. Railroad companies, for example, were extending their tracks westward from Chicago through Wisconsin and Minnesota into the Dakotas, Montana and the Pacific Northwest. For many Americans, track building was not worth the money offered or the sacrifice of resettling; but for recent arrivals and migrant workers, the money earned during a few weeks of working on the railroads outmatched that which could be earned during several months of grueling labor in the old country. Many Macedonians therefore flocked to Montana from Midwestern states. Setting track outside in the open country also beat laboring away in stuffy and dirty factories. Christowe even noted that working on this new expansive railroad project stirred feelings that the men were helping build America.

Other jobs also brought Macedonians to Montana, a large state rich in a variety of natural resources. At the turn of the century, Montana had been relatively unexplored and unexploited by European settlers. Throughout much of the 19th century, control of Montana had been contested and the only European-Americans setting foot there were associated with the fur trade. The first permanent European-American settlement was not established until the middle of the 19th century. In the last third of the century, however, explorers discovered large deposits of vital resources, such as gold, copper, silver and coal. Thus, at the turn of the 20th century, mining had exploded into a booming industry. These mining jobs, although dangerous and tough, attracted many Macedonians. Most of them found work in Butte's copper mines.

The majority of Macedonians who labored on the railroads or in the mines only spent a few years in Montana and returned to bustling Macedonian communities in the Midwest or brought their fortunes with them to Macedonia. Yet, several other Macedonians remained. They chose Montana precisely because it was Big Sky Country: the small population centers meant more space; the towns were quaint and cozy like their Macedonian villages, but lacked the poverty, anarchy and tyranny that was rampant in Macedonia; and the mountains were enormous, the rivers clean, and the valleys wide and green. Montana was paradise; the Midwestern cities were dirty, noisy and overwhelming. Montana reminded the Macedonian settlers of home absent the fear and suffering.

At least 2,000 Macedonians worked and lived in Montana in the first two decades of the 20th century.[4] This, however, is only an educated guess. The precise number is very difficult to calculate for a variety of reasons. First, we are limited by the types and quantity of official documents and records. The best available sources we have include the U.S. Census, which occurred only every 10 years; military records, such as World

War I Draft Registration Cards (herein referred to as WW1 Cards) and records of military service; marriage licenses; birth and death certificates; and newspaper articles. Because most Macedonians only lived and worked in Montana for a few years (or less), many did not make it onto any of these documents. For example, if a Macedonian was in Montana from 1911 through 1914, which was during the height of early Macedonian immigration to Montana, it is very likely that he would have never been recorded in any official document. (He would have likely been recorded in company archives of personnel files, but this presents its own problems, as we will see below.)

Second, many Macedonians were not recorded as being from Macedonia because Macedonia was not yet a country, even though many hundreds of Macedonians insisted that they came from Macedonia. Before the Balkan Wars of 1912 and 1913, Macedonia was an unofficial province of Turkey (the Ottoman Empire); thus, many Macedonians who immigrated before 1913 listed Turkey as their country of origin. After Macedonia was liberated from Turkey, it was then split and divided between Bulgaria, Greece and Serbia (the Serbian part eventually becoming a constituent republic of Yugoslavia and then today's Republic of Macedonia). Therefore, many Macedonians listed those countries as their countries of origin.

Third, searching for Macedonians solely based on given names and surnames is inefficient and often leads to inaccurate results. On one hand, several Macedonians assumed Americanized names (such as Tom Paul, Jim Pete, Mike Nick, Mike George, e.g.) when arriving in the U.S., rendering it difficult to distinguish between them and other Americans. Many others had names similar to those of neighboring peoples, such as Bulgarians and Serbians, which makes distinguishing between them nearly impossible (if birth locations were not given). Finally, some Macedonians switched between Serbianized, Bulgarianized, and Grecianized surnames depending on who possessed Macedonia. These reasons make searching through railroad company personnel records, for example, difficult when compounded with the fact that most of these records no longer exist and the indexes that exist do not necessarily include the employee's birth location.

Nevertheless, official records and newspapers provide a reliable and fruitful supply of data. When accounting for the above reasons, it is probable that well over 2,000 Macedonians worked and lived in Montana during the 20th century.[5] Some of these Macedonians made a lifetime commitment to Montana. The available evidence suggests that about 100 men decided to permanently settle in Montana and start families. A handful either remained single or continued supporting their families in Macedonia with hopes of eventually bringing them to America but failed in that respect. Most of these Macedonians, however, married non-Macedonians.

Based on available migration patterns within the U.S., the number of Americans with some portion of Macedonian ancestry in Montana today is probably around 500. Most of the first- and second-generation Macedonians have died and many of the younger generations have moved to larger cities on the West Coast. It is unknown how many of these descendants – whether or not still in Montana – identify as Macedonian-Americans or are aware of their Macedonian ancestry.

In this book, I examine 645 Macedonian-born individuals who lived and worked in Montana for a substantial period of time. I only included those who were listed, in at least one document, as hailing from Macedonia. In the first part of this book, I examine the data and trends to reach some conclusions about Macedonian immigration patterns in Montana. I also provide some anecdotes that help contextualize the Macedonian immigrant experience in Montana. In the second part of the book, I delve deeper into the lives of those Macedonians who decided to remain in Montana permanently. Just under 10% of these 645 Macedonians lived and died in

Montana, and I highlight their lives and their descendants' lives by providing some biographical profiles and interesting stories from their lives. This allows Macedonians and others to better understand how Macedonians adjusted to the New World and integrated into society in areas where large Macedonian colonies did not exist. Finally, the third part of this book is a list of 645 Macedonians, which includes their birth years and primary place of residence in Montana.

Although relatively a small population, Macedonians have spread to many different regions throughout the world. There are likely more Macedonians outside of Macedonia than in Macedonia today. A minor portion of these immigrants and *pechalbari* (migrant workers) ended up in Montana. It is my hope that this book contributes to the growing body of literature and studies on Macedonians in America.

# 1
## *Some Basic Facts and Trends*

**Birthplace.** The 645 Macedonians studied in this book were listed as being born in Macedonia in at least one official government document or newspaper article. Even though Macedonia did not gain official status as a constituent republic of Yugoslavia until after World War II, scores of these Macedonian immigrants to Montana in the first few decades of the 20th century declared Macedonia, and *only* Macedonia, as their country of birth. In total, about 325 of the studied 645 Macedonians listed *only* Macedonia as their country of birth, which is slightly over half of those examined. Although this percentage may not shock most Macedonians, who understand the extent to which the name 'Macedonia' was integral to their ancestors' lives, it is still an incredible figure given the historical circumstances and the official Greek and Bulgarian denial of the historical and present existence of Macedonians as a separate people.

Nearly all of these Macedonians came to Montana in the first two decades of the 20th century and at no point during that time was Macedonia ever an independent country. The fact that all of these individuals listed Macedonia as their birthplace in at least one document, and about half *only* listed Macedonia as their country of birth, demonstrates that a large number of Macedonians believed that Macedonia was a separate country (and especially separate from neighboring Bulgaria, Greece, Albania and Serbia if immigrating after 1913, which was when Macedonia was liberated from the Ottoman Empire and attached to neighboring countries) and that Macedonia constituted its own nation. These immigrants, who knew that Macedonia was divided under neighboring countries, probably hoped that Macedonia would eventually be freed. Regardless of their reasons, they were cognizant of the fact that

Macedonia was their homeland and that they had no other homeland. When asked what country they came from, Macedonia was usually the automatic response.

Still, about half of those in this study listed other countries as their birthplaces (such as Turkey, Greece, Bulgaria or Serbia) on separate documents or on the same document that listed Macedonia as their birthplace. For example, Lazar Nanoff had Florina, Turkey listed as his birthplace on his WWI Card,[6] while Alexander Dimitroff listed Kastoria, Macedonia, Greece as his birthplace on his WW1 Card.[7] These facts, however, do not necessarily mean that these immigrants did not view themselves as Macedonians or did not view Macedonia as a separate entity. For example, Christ Hlebaroff was described as originating from Vodena, Macedonia, Bulgaria on his WW1 Card.[8] He died in Montana in 1918, less than one year later, and his gravestone omits Bulgaria. Instead, it reads: "Born in Vodena, Macedonia."[9] So, what gives? Why, in less than a year, is Bulgaria omitted from his birthplace and the final expression of his birthplace is listed as *only* Macedonia, even though Macedonia was not an independent country at the time?

It is possible that a variety of factors could have determined why Hlebaroff and many other Macedonian immigrants to Montana (and to the entire U.S., for that matter) had other countries listed as their birthplaces. For starters, immigration officials and census enumerators had a job to do, which in part consisted of determining and recording the country of origin for immigrants. Some of these officials likely just wrote down what they heard: if someone said his country was Macedonia, then the official would record Macedonia. Many of these officials probably knew very little or nothing about Balkan politics or geography and had no reason (or will) to doubt an individual who said his country of birth was Macedonia.

More knowledgeable officials, however, would press for additional information. These officials may have known that

Macedonia was not a recognized country and took the time to determine from which officially recognized country these individuals originated. Yes, Kostur (Kastoria) was located in Macedonia; but before 1913, that part of Macedonia was located in Turkey and afterwards it became a part of Greece. It is plausible that an official would press an individual who insisted he was from Macedonia to provide another answer. Still, it was undoubtedly confusing for U.S. officials, as several Macedonians were recorded as being from more than one country and some others even had the names of several different countries crossed out on their documents.

To further complicate matters, many individuals' WWI Cards had different Balkan countries listed as their country of citizenship compared to their country of birth. For example, Vane Christoff, who was from Konomlati (Aegean Macedonia), listed Greece as his country of birth and Turkey as his country of citizenship on his WW1 Card,[10] despite the fact that Aegean Macedonia was no longer part of Turkey. Further, take the example of Tom Triff: in the 1920 U.S. Census, he was recorded as being from Macedonia, Greece,[11] but his WWI Card from three years prior listed him as a citizen of Bulgaria and his nearest living relative as residing in Macedonia, Turkey.[12] This inconsistency and confusion was indeed widespread amongst Macedonian immigrants during the early 20th century.

As I mentioned, one reason for this ambiguity is due to the fact that immigrants had to list something other than Macedonia if an official insisted Macedonia was not sufficient. However, there are two other potential reasons for this dilemma. The second is that many immigrants themselves likely had no idea, especially during the 1910s, which country ruled Macedonia. Three wars in the span of just six years had placed different parts of Macedonia under different rulers, and these parts of Macedonia exchanged hands several times during these wars. It was not known if Turkey, Bulgaria, Greece or Serbia controlled Macedonia or if Macedonia had potentially achieved independence, as many Macedonians surely hoped. Alexander Dimitroff of Kostur, who was living in Missoula in 1917, asked this question himself and the *Daily Missoulian* wrote a short article about it entitled, "A Man Without a Country." In part, it said:

**[Macedonia] has been changing rulers so often in the past few years that he [Dimitroff] was at a loss to say just who was controlling it now. The censorship, of course, did not aid his efforts at accuracy. When he left Macedonia, it was in the hands of Turks. Shortly afterwards, the first Balkan War occurred, and Bulgaria took over the province. Then came the second Balkan war and the Greeks gained control of Macedonia.**[13]

That article was written during World War I, a war in which Macedonia saw a variety of foreign armies march through its land. Even in today's modern age of instant communication, it is often difficult to determine the truth of matters in faraway war-torn countries; in early 20th century Macedonia, it was even that much more difficult.

A third possibility centers around the treatment of immigrants in the U.S. during World War I. Men from Germany and her allies were considered enemy aliens in the U.S. and were thus forbidden from carrying firearms or serving in the U.S. military. Bulgaria was aligned with Germany during the war. It is entirely feasible that some Macedonians figured out that listing Bulgaria as their birthplace, even if their village was located in Vardar Macedonia (Serbian Macedonia) or Aegean Macedonia (Greek Macedonia), might exempt them from military service. If one's birthplace was listed as Macedonia, the he could still escape service in the war so long as he declared that he was a citizen of Bulgaria.[14]

Any three of these reasons could explain why Christ Hlebaroff and other Macedonians listed Bulgaria as their country of birth on their WWI Cards. Perhaps some felt that Macedonia should indeed be part of Bulgaria. But for Christ

Hlebaroff, that he was from Macedonia and felt that he was *only* from Macedonia is evidenced by the fact that only Macedonia, and not Bulgaria, is engraved on his tombstone.

Modern Bulgaria generally argues that Macedonia belonged to Bulgaria historically and that most people in geographic Macedonia historically believed they were Bulgarians and/or that Macedonia belonged to Bulgaria. If this assertion was a truth, however, then the official records should so more Macedonian immigrants declaring Bulgaria as their birthplace. Half of those examined in this study declared that they were *only* from Macedonia despite Macedonia not officially existing as an independent country and instead distributed between Turkey, Serbia, Greece and Bulgaria. This bold proclamation could, at least for some, indicate that they did not recognize any fatherland or homeland other than Macedonia. If Macedonians instead felt that Bulgaria was their homeland, we would then expect to see many more individuals put *only* Bulgaria as their homeland.

Perhaps there are some Macedonians not included in this study, due to an inability to verify their birthplace, that put they were only from Bulgaria. But based on the data for the other half of Macedonians who have countries other than Macedonia listed on some other document, it is highly unlikely that Bulgaria would have been the country of choice for most Macedonians. Of those Macedonians who had other Balkan countries listed as their birthplaces on other documents, about 60% listed Turkey as their birthplace and just over 30% listed Greece as a birthplace. Only 12% listed Bulgaria as a birthplace and a handful indicated Serbia or Yugoslavia. (The numbers do not add up to 100% because some individuals had two or three different countries listed as birthplaces on different documents). It is likely that most Macedonians who have gone unexamined in this study probably listed Turkey or Greece as their birthplaces. Patriotism for Bulgaria thus was practically irrelevant.

**Language.** The strongest case Bulgarian propagandists have for demonstrating the ethnic or political allegiances of Macedonian immigrants relates to the issue of language. Out of the 645 individuals examined, we have information from at least one document (mostly U.S. Census records) on the language spoken of 416 Macedonians. The mother tongues for these individuals were listed as follows: Bulgarian, 192; Turkish, 124; Macedonian, 70; Romanian, 13; Greek, 11; Slavic, 4; Latin, 1; and one individual is listed as speaking several of the above languages. *Figure A* below provides a visualization of the listed mother tongues for these Macedonian immigrants.

### Figure A

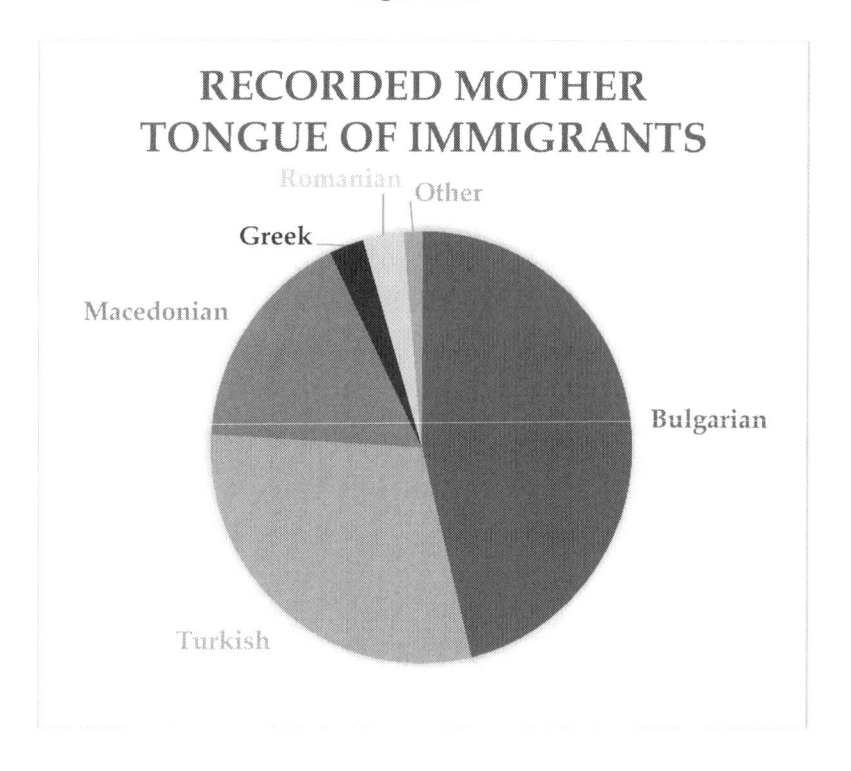

### RECORDED MOTHER TONGUE OF IMMIGRANTS

(Pie chart showing: Bulgarian, Turkish, Macedonian, Greek, Romanian, Other)

One reason why many Macedonians are listed as speaking Bulgarian relates to Balkan politics of the time. The Macedonian language was not codified until the 1940s, even though several Macedonian scholars and activists in the 19th and early 20th century advocated for its codification, such as Gjorgji Pulevski (who in 1875 published a book called *Dictionary of Three Languages*, which examined Macedonian, Albanian and Turkish), and Krste Misirkov (who made the case for a separate Macedonian language in many articles and in his 1903 book *On Macedonian Matters*). For much of the Turkish Empire's existence in the Balkans, Greek was the primary non-Turkish language utilized for commerce and in the church because Greeks had a monopoly over all Orthodox Christians in Turkey. When Bulgaria gained its autonomy, it started pushing for Bulgarian schools and churches to be opened in Macedonia. Macedonian dialects, which fall under the Slavic language family, are much more closely related to Bulgarian (a Slavic language) than to Greek. Therefore, it was easy for Macedonian pupils to apply the Bulgarian terminology to their language or to understand the Bulgarian language. In addition, Bulgarian political elements showed more willingness than other Balkan peoples to assist the Macedonians in achieving autonomy from Turkey, which forged a closer bond between many Macedonians and Bulgarians than with Greeks or Serbians. These factors contributed significantly as to why Macedonians declared (or were recorded as declaring) that they used the Bulgarian language.

Of course, there are other reasons why Bulgarian appeared so often compared to Macedonian. It is likely that U.S. officials would press Macedonians to give an officially recognized language because Macedonian was not recognized or codified, similar to how Macedonia was not recognized as a country and officials would press to obtain an answer that satisfied that question's purpose. As a matter of fact, before the 1910 U.S. Census, Albert Sonnichsen (who had spent time in the Balkans) advised his fellow Americans not to distinguish between Macedonians and Bulgarians with regards to race or language. He said, in part:

> **I hope you are not making any racial distinctions between Bulgars and Macedonians. I believe the Bulgarians who have come from Macedonia are registered on Ellis Island as Macedonians, which is bound to be confusing and inaccurate, for Macedonians may include Greeks, Vlachs and even Turks. The distinction between Bulgars from Bulgaria and those from Macedonia is purely political. Many of those who are registered as Greeks are so in church affiliation only, being Slavic by race and tongue.**[15]

However, Sonnichsen also warned against labeling all these Macedonian immigrants as being from Bulgaria and that the speech between immigrants from Bulgaria and those from Macedonia could be distinguished. He stated:

> **There is as much difference in speech and intonation as between Missouri and County Clare [Ireland], though the Bulgarian of Bulgarian schools and Macedonian schools is the same.**[16]

Still, though, he and others spread the misconception that the dialects spoken by Macedonian immigrants should be called Bulgarian.

Although Sonnichsen's views were not the only ones to sway public opinion in the U.S., they had an effect. The instructions to census enumerators in 1910 omitted Macedonian as an official language and instead instructed the enumerators to "not write 'Macedonian,' but write Bulgarian, Turkish, Greek, Servian, or Roumanian, as the case may be."[17] A decade later, however, in the instructions to enumerators for the 1920 U.S. Census, Macedonian was listed as one of 63 principal languages that were "likely to be reported as the mother tongue or language of customary speech of foreign-born persons[,]" and in the 1930 U.S. Census, Macedonian was one among 59 principal languages. Macedonian was not yet codified, but it was no longer banned from being recorded in the U.S. Census.[18] Moreover, the instructions for both the 1930 and 1940 U.S. Census enumerators insisted that "mother tongue is not necessarily the same as the language of the country in which the person was born"[19] and that 'Slavic' was not an acceptable language.[20]

It is thus remarkable that about 17% of Macedonians did indeed put that they spoke Macedonian, and this insistence that they only spoke Macedonian must have persuaded U.S. officials to accept Macedonian as a language even though it was not a codified language. As children, many Macedonians had been exposed to propaganda that categorized their language as Bulgarian and some Americans and Balkan propagandists made compelling arguments to U.S. officials on how to interpret 'Macedonian'. These 70 Macedonians working in Montana who listed Macedonian as their mother tongue, however, are not marginal: their act cannot be written off as a fluke. It is another sign of strengthening Macedonian patriotism and identity in the early 20th century. That about 46% of these Macedonians were listed as speaking Bulgarian and 30% as Turkish is in no small part due to Balkan propaganda and official U.S. policy; that 17% insisted they spoke Macedonian was significant enough to have an impact on U.S. policy on Balkan languages and, unknowingly, support the case for an already established Macedonian identity in the early 20th century, several decades before Bulgaria and Greece insist that an 'artificial Macedonian ethnic identity' was created.

Moreover, the declaration of one's language as Macedonian can truly be seen as a conscious or deliberate affirmation of a Macedonian ethnic identity and not merely expression of a strong regional identity, as Bulgarians and Greeks often insist. Out of all the 70 Macedonians who declared Macedonian to be their mother tongue, none of them were listed as being born in Bulgaria in any official documents and only 11 of them had Turkey or Greece listed as a birthplace on a document. This suggests that those who were documented as speaking Macedonian did not look to Bulgaria as their homeland. Meanwhile, only 14 out of the 192 Macedonians (7%) who were described as speaking Bulgarian had Bulgaria listed as their birthplace on any other of their documents. This helps demonstrate that, even if one viewed his language as Bulgarian (whether or not because of the aforementioned reasons), he did not necessarily view himself as a Bulgarian and was certainly not a Bulgarian patriot.

**Age and Immigration Year.** While there is little information on when these immigrants came to Montana, these Macedonian men (only a handful were women) primarily came to the U.S. in the first two decades of the century. Out of the 269 individuals for which their first immigration year is known, 261 came between 1901 and 1919. However, this tells only one part of the story: just nine had arrived before 1906 and only eight arrived after 1917. The years with the most numerous Macedonians immigrants are as follows: 1916, 68; 1912, 31; 1907, 29; 1914, 26; and 1910, 19. _Figure B_ below illustrates the immigration trends.

**Figure B**

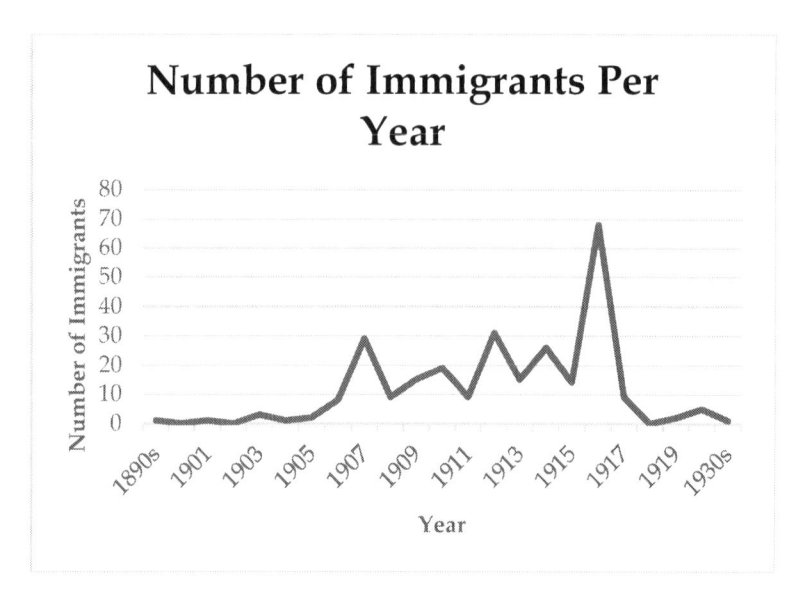

Number of Immigrants Per Year

A look at these numbers would seem to suggest that most Macedonians came to the U.S. in the early to mid-1910s. However, these numbers do not necessarily tell the whole story. For example, this study does not examine data on those Macedonians who may have had *only* Turkey listed as their birthplace. Being that all of Macedonia was located within Turkey from the 14th century through 1913, it is likely that many Macedonians who came before 1913 would have listed Turkey as their country of birth. This number is probably unverifiable, but the lack of this information likely skews our sample of Macedonian immigrants toward having immigrated in the 1910s rather than in the 1900s.

Still, the information we do have can certainly highlight some correlations. First, the fact that the overwhelming majority of immigrants (95%) that immigrated in this time period were men helps demonstrate that most of these men were not fleeing wars or political persecution. Certainly, wars and persecution drove tens of thousands of Macedonians out of their homeland, with most of them fleeing to safety in neighboring Bulgaria, Serbia and Greece or other European countries. They usually fled with their families if escaping war or by themselves if fleeing political persecution. If the Macedonians arriving in the U.S. were war refugees, then we would expect to see many more women and children in this sample.

This assumption is further corroborated by the fact that the years that saw the most immigration do not correlate with significant violent periods in Macedonia's 20th century history. For example, the Macedonians rebelled against the Turkish Sultan's forces in summer and autumn of 1903, a rebellion that included thousands of armed rebels, hundreds of battles, and an excess of massacring, pillaging and razing of villages through the winter of 1904. Thousands of refugees were reported as fleeing into Bulgaria, indeed. However, we see a relatively flat immigration trend to the U.S. from 1903 until

1906. While it might be easy to attribute this low immigration level to the assumption that many Macedonian immigrants during these years reported Turkey and not Macedonia as their birthplace, it is not that clear. Macedonia was also a part of Turkey until 1913, and the years between 1907 and 1912 saw much more immigration than between 1903 and 1906. And while it is entirely possible that Macedonians were becoming more patriotic and identifying as Macedonian because of the 1903 insurrection, this does not necessarily explain the trend.

Moreover, the Balkan Wars began in the autumn of 1912 and lasted through the summer of 1913. While we see a significant jump in immigration of Macedonians in 1912, we see a substantial decrease in Macedonian immigration in 1913. We then see another substantial increase in immigration in 1914 – well after the wars were over. On top of that, parts of Macedonia (especially Vardar Macedonia) were dragged into the First World War in the autumn of 1915 and in more intensity throughout 1916. In 1916, we do see the greatest number of Macedonian immigrants. However, the war lasted until the autumn of 1918, and 1917 and 1918 saw some of the lowest levels of immigration. Thus, fleeing war cannot be the primary explanation for this level of Macedonian immigration.

It is more probable that men were less likely to immigrate during wartime because they were recruited into armies or volunteered to fight. Many Macedonians actually traveled back to Macedonia to fight in the Balkan Wars and World War I. (For example, in a one-week span during the First Balkan War, 1,000 Macedonians and other Balkan natives left Granite City for the Balkans.)[21] Also, we see many Macedonians immigrating to the U.S. in 1906 and 1907 and then see a sharp decline in 1908 and 1909. In 1907, about 30 Macedonians immigrated while in 1908 that number dropped to 10 and creeped back up slightly to 15 in 1909. This decrease is possibly due to the Young Turk Uprising in Turkey, which promised better conditions, reforms and more rights for Macedonians and other Christians, as well as the removal of the Sultan from the throne. With the prospects of government reform likely came hope of improving economic and lifestyle standards.

A similar reason could be used to explain the increase in immigrants in 1903 and the decrease in 1904. After the Macedonian 1903 Ilinden Uprising, Turkey was compelled by some of the Great Powers to institute reforms that were intended to improve conditions for the Macedonian Christians. These reforms were, in part, intended to finally give Macedonians assurances that the provisions of the Berlin Treaty from over a quarter of a century prior would be realized. It could be that less Macedonians immigrated due to an anticipation that these reforms would change Macedonia's economic and social conditions. However, our sampling size is too small to reach such a conclusion. More, the evidence suggests that Macedonian immigration to the U.S. did not reach any meaningful numbers until after 1903, which would make comparing numbers of immigrants in 1904 and 1902, for example, futile.

What is true is that these men, whenever they came, were mostly *pechalbari* who made their way to the U.S. for a brief period (or for multiple brief periods) and eventually returned home. The economic stagnation, high taxes, wars, and anarchy in Turkish Macedonia created intolerable and miserable financial situations for most peasants. When word reached villages that fortunes were to be made in America, these poor peasants shipped out by the hundreds. A Macedonian could make much more money in a month in the U.S. than in a year in Macedonia. While most men did not know what awaited them in the U.S., there was at least some hope to be had in the U.S: in Macedonia, hope had been essentially extinguished.

It is also unlikely that U.S. immigration policies had a significant impact on Macedonian immigration. True, the U.S. Immigration Act of 1917 (implemented in its final form in February of 1917) severely limited the number of immigrants admitted into the U.S. by banning a variety of undesirables, including anarchists, idiots, political radicals, and illiterates, among other categories. That which affected the Macedonians the most would have been the illiterate category. The new law required immigrants over the age 16 to read a few sentences in their native language. Because the vast majority of Macedonians were illiterate during this time period (and the literacy rate hardly rose prior to the 1930s),[22] this new law would have likely served as a serious impediment for Macedonians. As a matter of fact, we see immigration slip from 69 in 1916 to under 10 in 1917.

While we know that the First World War was raging in 1917, we do not know if such drastic decrease in immigration levels is due to this immigration law, Macedonian men being recruited into or volunteering for armies, or a combination of the two. However, the U.S. went on to impose immigration quotas on Eastern European and Southern European countries between 1921 and 1924. These quotas certainly must have impacted Macedonian immigration to the U.S. Still, for the variations in immigration numbers we see between 1903 and 1916, U.S. immigration policies likely had little effect on the variation in numbers we see in-between those years.

When these immigrants first arrived in the U.S., they varied widely in age and birth date. Out of the 645 Macedonians analyzed here, the year of birth is known for 576 of them. It should be noted, though, that when I say the year of birth is known, I mean that year of birth is listed in at least one document. When most of these Macedonians were born, no official recordkeeping existed and peasants did not keep track of their birthdays. Thus, the birth years provided here are estimates by either the immigrants themselves or U.S. government officials, and some of the immigrants have different ages listed on different documents. Thus, the birth years are not always accurate.

Still, the listed birth years can be considered to be relatively close to an immigrant's actual birth year based on the fact that the differing birthdates for an immigrant were usually no more than 3 or 4 years apart. As *Figure C* below shows, 227 of the individuals, or about 39%, were born in the 1880s. This is 6 percentage points more than those born in the 1890s (191) and about twice the amount born in the 1870s (114). In relation to historical Macedonian events, most of these men would have not fought or participated in the Ilinden Uprising of 1903, but they would have been completely aware and immersed into the Internal Macedonian Revolutionary Organization (IMRO) culture.

**Figure C**

**NUMBER OF MACEDONIAN IMMIGRANTS PER BIRTH DECADE**

| Birth Decade | Number of Immigrants |
|---|---|
| 1850s | 1 |
| 1860s | 27 |
| 1870s | 114 |
| 1880s | 227 |
| 1890s | 191 |
| 1900s | 13 |
| 1910s | 3 |

However, in order to better put these immigrants' birth years in context, we are best served by understanding their age at arrival. While we have birth years for 576 of these immigrants and immigration years for only 261 of them, we know both the birth year and immigration year for 254 of them. This number provides us with enough data to make some noteworthy observations. The average age at immigration was 26.8 years old; the median age was 24; and the ages that these Macedonians most frequently arrived in the U.S. were 16 (18 individuals) and 19 (16 individuals). The oldest immigrant was 57 years old and the youngest was four.

However, we can further better understand these numbers in another way: by looking at the data for specific years, especially those years with higher immigration levels. For example, in 1916, the year which saw the largest number of Macedonians immigrants in this sample, the statistical information is different from the overall sample. For 1916, the average age at immigration is 32, which is more than five years older than the average for the entire sample; the median is 28, which is four years higher than the overall median; and the most frequent ages of immigration are 16 and 31, both with five. However, we see the reverse trend for those immigrants who came nearly ten years prior in 1907. The average age for this sample was 22.9, almost four years younger than the overall sample; the median age was 20, which is also four years less than the overall sample median age; and the most frequent ages of immigration are 16 and 19, which is equal to the overall sample.

To further detail this trend, *Figure D* on the following page graphs the average age for immigrants per year in that range of years where we see substantial immigration, 1906 to 1916. Essentially, this demonstrates that as the years go by, the age at first immigration year increases.

## Figure D

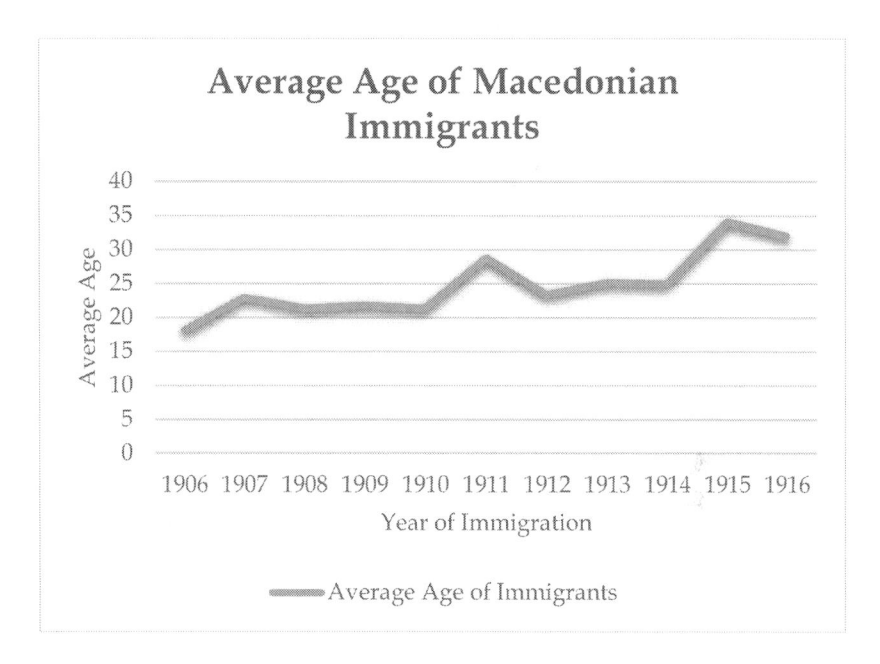

**Average Age of Macedonian Immigrants**

(Graph showing Average Age on the y-axis from 0 to 40, and Year of Immigration on the x-axis from 1906 to 1916. Legend: Average Age of Immigrants.)

It is worthwhile to note that while the average age at immigration goes up throughout the ten-year period, it is not a steady increase. What we see are essentially three significantly meaningful jumps in age of immigration with two relatively flat segments in-between. So, why does this trend exist? Why were the Macedonians who immigrated later in this time period older? What explains these jumps?

First, something that must be accounted for is that underage children without a guardian would nearly always claim that they were older; otherwise, they faced deportation. However, it is unlikely that this would have been more common in the 1915 than in 1908. It is likely, although, that younger men and teenagers were more willing to take risks: they were more curious and/or able to make it out West. Once the elders saw the money and material items these youngsters were acquiring, they also became intrigued and tempted by the New World. Still, the older men had farms and households to tend; younger men (especially those who were unmarried) did not have that same responsibility and commitment.

Another noteworthy observation is that the two years in which we see a significant drop-off in the average age of immigration are years of heavy war and fighting after a relatively stable year of peace. For example, in 1911, the average age of immigrants is 29, but in 1912, the year the First Balkan War began, the average age of immigration is about 24. Or, in 1915 the average age is 34, and then by the time Macedonian became extensively involved in World War I in 1916, the average age drops down to 32. Perhaps the older and more capable men remained in Macedonia to fight.

Then again, perhaps the numbers are just a fluke. Still, it is significant that, in an 11-year span, the average age of immigrants nearly doubled.

**Where they moved to in Montana.** Most Macedonians' first destination was not Montana. Many settled in Indiana, Ohio and Illinois before heading out West. However, when they came to Montana, they worked and lived throughout the entire state. The most common areas where Macedonians lived include Lombard, Rosebud, Dawson, Butte, Warland, Fergus, Miles City, and Deer Lodge. As we will see below, many of these places were temporary living quarters because Macedonians were working on the railroads. The Macedonians who remained in Montana for the rest of their lives generally lived in Butte, Missoula, Miles City and Great Falls.

*Figure E* on the next page is a sketch of Montana that shows the eight locations with the largest concentrations of Macedonians in Montana. This demonstrates the extent to which large numbers of Macedonians were spread throughout the entire state. (Some locations are cities while others are settlements or counties, and those with the larger dots indicate a higher concentration of Macedonians.)

## Figure E
## Largest Concentrations of Macedonians in Montana

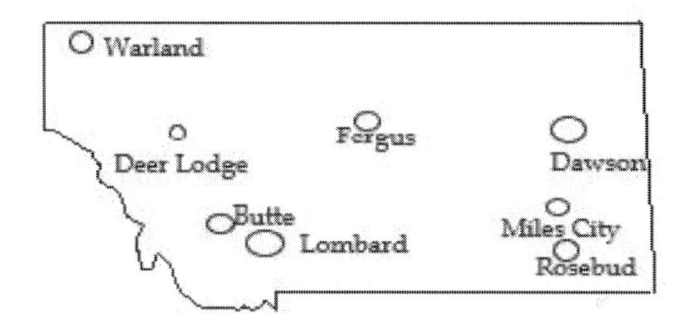

*Figure F* on the following page charts where Macedonians in Montana lived during their time there (the places of residence for 632 out of the 645 Macedonian immigrants studied are known). The places of residence are arranged alphabetically. Those classified as 'Other' come from 60 locations where there were less than five Macedonians residing. These 632 Macedonians were dispersed over 87 different locations (although there may be some overlap, as some given locations are counties while others are cities that may be located in those counties).

## Figure F
## Where Macedonian Immigrants Resided in Montana

| Location | Number of Macedonians |
|---|---|
| Armington | 20 |
| Bearmouth | 8 |
| Bowdoin | 9 |
| Box Elder | 10 |
| Butte | 39 |
| Cascade | 6 |
| Charlo | 21 |
| Chinook | 8 |
| Chouteau | 5 |
| Corbin | 9 |
| Cottonwood | 13 |
| Dawson | 49 |
| Deer Lodge | 24 |
| Fergus | 34 |
| Great Falls | 16 |
| Lewiston | 8 |
| Lombard | 65 |
| Meagher | 19 |
| Miles City | 30 |
| Missoula | 19 |
| Rosebud | 35 |
| Saltese | 7 |
| Superior | 9 |
| Warland | 34 |
| Whitefish | 5 |
| Wolf Point | 5 |
| Yellowstone | 10 |
| Other (60 locations) | 115 |
| **Total** | **632** |

What these numbers ultimately show is that Macedonians in Montana were not clustered or congregated to the same extent that they were in other states during the first two or three decades of the 20$^{th}$ century. While Macedonians in Michigan were generally in Detroit, Battle Creek, Kalamazoo and Lansing, and Macedonians in New York were generally located in Buffalo, Rochester and Syracuse, the Macedonians in Montana were working and living in scores of different settlements and cities throughout the entire state. This is, in no small part, due to the employment situation in Montana, as we will see below.

The impact that this had on the formation of a permanent Macedonian colony, however, was significant. First, most employment was temporary and mobile, meaning many Macedonians were on the move and never lingered for too long in one area. Second, Montana is a large state; even though many cities and settlements contained Macedonians, they each had a relatively small number (compared to cities in the Midwest where Macedonians settled). The distances between those settlements were relatively large. This likely affected the Macedonians' ability to become an established colony in any of these areas.

**Employment**. Why do we see such a large number of residences for such a relatively small population size? The essential reason is that Macedonians came to Montana fleetingly for the railroad jobs. Railroads were being constructed throughout the entire state and the laborers were constantly moving westward or northward as the tracks were laid and secured. The Great Northern Railway was the most common railroad that Macedonians worked on, which extended through most of northern and central Montana. However, other Macedonians worked on different railway lines in southern, eastern and western Montana. Of the 568 known occupations of the Macedonians studied herein, 497 of them (87.5%) worked on the railroads.

Most Macedonians worked as section laborers. Often times, the foreman would be a U.S. born individual. However, where there were large gangs of Macedonians working as laborers, they often would put a Macedonian in charge of the group, called a section foreman. Many of these Macedonians who served as section foremen would remain in Montana for the rest of their lives, such as Nick Thompson, who immigrated in 1907 and spent much time in Teton County and Great Falls;[23] James Christoff, who was a section leader in Benton Township and Bowdoin;[24] and Lee Angeloff, who was a section foreman in 1940 at Hedgesville, where he resided with his Macedonian-born wife, Anna.[25] These Macedonian foremen, along with many others, were more likely (per capita, compared to regular section laborers) to remain in Montana. Perhaps the pay was better; perhaps the responsibility and role made them feel more fulfilled and integral to their work and place in society.

While construction of railroads brought most Macedonians to Montana, there were two other fields that Macedonians primarily occupied: farming and mining. Probably because farming was the livelihood of most Macedonian peasants in the old country, many were able to transition into farming in Montana with relative ease. Twenty of these 645 men were listed as farmers. Some of them include James (John) Tricoff, who lived in Montana from the 1910s until his death in 1975 and spent most of his working years as a farmer in the Butte region;[26] Christ D. Botaff, who lived in Montana since the 1910s and worked in Whitefish as a farmer for over three decades before his death in 1962;[27] and Tony Gechoff, who was recorded in the 1940 U.S. Census as working as a farmer and living in Miles City.[28] Like railroad section foremen, those who farmed were usually Macedonians who remained in Montana until death. Many also had previous jobs (such as in railroad building) but decided to settle down in Montana and make a home and family.

Sixteen of these 645 men worked as miners, mostly in the copper mines. Most of these men worked in the mines around Butte, which was notorious for its copper mines in Montana. For example, Nass Naumoff was recorded as working there in 1930;[29] Metody Batchoff worked as a miner in Butte from 1912 until his death in 1932;[30] and Theodore Mano mined in Butte's copper mines from 1924 until his death in 1949.[31] While there were other mines scattered throughout Montana, most Macedonian miners found themselves in Butte and remained there throughout their lives.

Of course, the remaining 35 Macedonians dabbled in all sorts of other occupations. One was a bartender. Pete George was recorded as bartending in a hotel in Missoula during the 1940 U.S. Census.[32] While he is the only bartender recorded in this study, Stoyan Christowe, in his memoir *The Eagle and the Stork*, mentions in passing how he ran into a man from his village who worked as a bartender at Park Hotel, across from the railroad station in Great Falls.[33] It is possible that Christowe's bartender and Pete George are the same person: he could have moved the 165 miles to Missoula in the 25 years that had passed since Christowe saw him.

Other types of employment in which Macedonians found themselves engaged included working as cooks, bakers, barbers, shoe shiners, carpenters, loggers, smelters, and janitors. One Macedonian – Angelo Angilofsky – even bought, sold and traded animal hides.[34] Another, Dimitre Batchoff, who entrenched himself in the social and political life of Montana, would go on to be appointed by President Truman as U.S. Marshal for the entire state of Montana.[35] Railroad construction was by far the most common occupation, but it was not the only one.

**Military Service.** Many of these Macedonians working and residing in Montana lived there when the First World War began. The draft registration for World War I provides us with some important biographical information for these Macedonians. But these military records also show us that several of these men ended up being recruited into the U.S. military and had to serve their new country overseas. These migrant workers – many who had no intention of staying in the U.S., and some who probably escaped military service in the Balkans during the 1910s – now had to lay down their lives for a foreign country. Still, this was a foreign country that brought them more wealth, opportunity and freedom than they had ever experienced before, and some were more than willing to give up their lives to fight for the United States. Surely, some may have even hoped that a U.S. victory would mean freedom for their native Macedonia.

Below is a list that briefly outlines the military service of several Macedonians living in Montana during World War I. Some of the Macedonian immigrants who served in the military are examined in further detail in the next chapter and are thus omitted from the following list.

- Nick Andanoff, Rosebud, served between April and November of 1918.[36]
- Nikolif Simonoff, St. Regis, enlisted on December 14, 1917 at the age of 29; served as a private and honorably discharged on February 18, 1918.[37]
- Blagoye D. Mitsareff, Glasgow, enlisted in the army on June 25, 1918 at the age of 28; served overseas in the summer of 1919 and was honorably discharged.[38]
- Nick Serbinoff, Missoula, entered the military on August 30, 1917 at the age of 27; he never went overseas and was discharged on May 31, 1919.[39]
- Costa G. Pariza, Butte, entered military service on July 2, 1918 at the age of 29 and was discharged on December 29, 1918.[40] (Costa died in Butte 1987 after a long career in the Anaconda Minerals mines; he never married.)[41]
- Christ Sotir, Butte, entered the military on May 27, 1918 at 27 years old; discharged in February of 1919.[42]
- Christ Eftinoff, Miles City, enlisted on June 30, 1918 at the age of 29; discharged on December 18, 1918.[43]
- Philip Tanas, Great Falls, entered military service on July 26, 1918 at the age of 25; honorably discharged on December 9, 1918.[44]

- Spiro T. Malisory, St. Regis, was 24 when he enlisted into the military on September 18, 1917; discharged on April 2, 1918 for erroneous induction.[45]
- Pano T. Yosivoff, Melstone, entered military service on April 26, 1918 at the age of 28; served overseas from July 1918 through April 1919 and honorably discharged on May 3, 1919. (Pano was born in Prilep, Macedonia.)[46]
- Nick George, Lewiston, was 28 when he enlisted into the military in September of 1917; served overseas from July 14, 1918 to March 30, 1919 and was honorably discharged on April 20, 1919.[47]
- Ted G. Christ, Cascade, enlisted into the military at 23 years of age on May 29, 1918; served overseas from October 6, 1918 through May 14, 1919, when he was discharged.[48]
- Peter Pappas, Billings, joined the military on April 29, 1918 at the age of 22; discharged on September 26, 1919. (Peter was born in Bitola, Macedonia.)[49]
- Vasil Aleexoff, Billings, enlisted in the military in February of 1918 at the age of 26; died overseas due to pneumonia on June 28, 1918; survivors included his wife, Anastia Tetrova Aleexoff, in Aegean Macedonia.[50]
- Stasho G. Zugloff, Missoula, entered service on November 3, 1917 at the age of 23; honorably discharged in March of 1918. (Stasho was born in Vembell, Aegean Macedonia.)[51]
- Tom Basil, Bearmouth, joined the U.S. military on October 7, 1917 at the age of 22; served overseas from March 14, 1918 until February 3, 1919 when he died due to complications of tuberculosis and pneumonia.[52]
- Svetco Evanoff, Great Falls, entered military service in September of 1917 at the age of 36 and was discharged in March of 1919. (Svetco was born in Ohrid, Macedonia.)[53]

- Gust Chreest, Helena, served overseas with the U.S. military from August 1918 through July 1919. (Gust was born in Kostur, Macedonia.)[54]

**Identity and Community.** As noted throughout this chapter, Macedonians faced obstacles to forging a Macedonian community in Montana and in upholding their Macedonian identity for two primary reasons. First, most Macedonians worked on the railroads, which kept them constantly moving throughout the state (and due to the nature of the work being temporary). Second, and very much related to the first, Macedonians resided in nearly 90 different locations throughout Montana, which disconnected the dispersed Macedonians from other Macedonian concentrations. This combination resulted in Montana's permanent Macedonian residents having little access to many of their Macedonian brethren.

Of course, as Christowe noted, for those Macedonians who temporarily worked on the railroads together, their Macedonian connection allowed them to tolerate much of their situation with ease. For the few years they worked in Montana, they were able to keep their sense of community: most hardly knew English and would rarely venture into Montanan towns without the accompaniment of their compatriots. However, even for those Macedonians who remained, it is likely that their Macedonian upbringing and culture did not evaporate suddenly; and even more, there were attempts to uphold connection to their homeland and culture. There are plenty of examples.

For instance, Nurmi George died in Missoula in January of 1941 after 35 years of work in the U.S. Pallbearers at his funeral included some Macedonians and other individuals from the Balkans, such as George Regis, Marion Mincoff, Pete Shungaris, George Paulos, Alec Evanoff, and William Dimitroff.[55] Even though most Macedonian migrant workers were long gone from Montana and only a few hundred remained scattered throughout the state, there were enough Macedonians and other Balkan peoples to keep the community connections alive, as evidenced by their attendance at Nurmi's funeral.

Moreover, while there were not enough Macedonians in Montana for these Macedonians to form their own church, many remained close with their Macedonian and Balkan community by attending other Orthodox churches, especially the Serbian and Greek churches. Blage and Pana Eloff celebrated their 50th wedding anniversary together in 1971 at the Holy Trinity Serbian Orthodox Church of Butte;[56] funeral services for Metody Batchoff in 1932 were held at that same Serbian church;[57] Nick Thompson of Great Falls was a member of the Greek Orthodox Church in the area;[58] and a Greek Orthodox priest officiated Sultana Gamell's funeral in Denton in 1943.[59] These Macedonians and many others who lived near Orthodox churches attended them to both remain connected to their Orthodox faith and to other Macedonians and their Macedonian culture. Had there been more such churches throughout other parts of Montana, it is likely that Macedonians in those areas would have frequented them.

While church attendance and pallbearers at a funeral can indicate attachment to their Macedonian and Balkan community and culture, they admittedly do not speak directly to an individual's sense of Macedonian identity. But the records do show such attachment of Macedonians to their identity, even late into the 20th century. For example, take Matrona Angeloff, who died in Miles City in April of 1991 at the age of 90. Although she was legally known as Matrona Angeloff, her tombstone reads, "Matrona Makedonski Angeloff."[60] What better statement can be made about one's Macedonian identity than including the word 'Makedonski' (which essentially means 'Macedonian') on one's gravestone?

These Macedonian-Montanans show that, even several thousand miles away in a large state with few Macedonians, there was a desire to preserve and remain connected to their Macedonian heritage and identity. The Macedonians who remained in Big Sky Country may not have been the most visible community, but they never desired to shake off their Macedonians roots or identity. Rather, they preserved it to the greatest extent possible given the circumstances.

# 2

# *Profiles and Biographies of Macedonian-Montanans*

In this chapter, I explore the lives of several dozens of these Macedonian immigrants in further detail. For some, extensive information is known and a relatively comprehensive biography is provided. For others, less is known and I instead furnish brief overviews or snippets of their past. This list does not include profiles for all of the Macedonian-born immigrants who settled permanently in Montana; however, it does paint a picture of what life was like for Macedonians in Montana. Some became very successful, with gainful employment and happy families; others suffered depression and lived alone until their death in Montana. Their profiles are explored here in order to put a human element to the data and trends examined in the first chapter.

## **Lee and Anna Angeloff**

Lee and Anna (née Kostova) were both born in Turie, Macedonia: Lee in 1889, and Anna in 1898 (to parents Kosta and Mitra Lazarov). Lee first came to the U.S. in 1903 and returned to Macedonia a few years later. When he returned to the U.S. in 1908, he quickly found work for the Great Northern in 1909 and was sent to Hedgesville in 1910. He revisited Macedonia in 1912 and married Anna in May of that year. Lee left his expecting bride in Macedonia and returned to America to continue earning money on the railroads. While there, he was sent to work in Yellowstone. But back in Macedonia, his 5-year old son, Constantine, had died following a brief illness.

Lee was promoted to section foreman in 1919. His job took him to Musselshell in 1920, and he then wrote for Anna to join him in Montana. Within a year she arrived and became a U.S. citizen by 1925. In Montana, they started anew, settling in Hedgesville, where they raised three children: Ivan, Wesley, and Ellen. Lee died in July of 1956, after having worked for the Great Northern for 42 years. He is buried in Harlowton Cemetery. Anna died 34 years later in July of 1990. Although she had moved to California in 1962 to be with Ellen and Wesley, who had moved there shortly after their fathers' death, she is also buried in Harlowton Cemetery.[61]

Prior to their deaths, however, their son Ivan was killed at the age of 25 in an airplane accident in California in 1947. Ivan had been working for Fairchild Aerial Survey at the time and had just returned from a business trip in the eastern states. Ivan was occupied as the mechanic and flight engineer, having received his training at the Curtiss-Wright Technical School in Glendale, California. Shortly after graduating from there he began working for Consolidated Aircraft Company in California, where he had been given assignments around the world, such as in Australia, New Guinea and Hawaii. In 1946, he began working for Fairchild and had been stationed in Venezuela for several months prior to his death. One week before the plane crashed, he surprised his parents by visiting them in Montana.[62]

## Nick and Matrona Angeloff

Nick was born in Macedonia in 1895 and came to America at a young age. Since arriving in the U.S., he had longed to become an American citizen. In November of 1927, that dream became reality and he was awarded citizenship in Miles City. Before that, however, he had gone back to Macedonia and found himself a wife, Matrona "Makedonski," who was born in 1901. She left her village for Montana and together she and Nick started a family, raising a son named Pete and a daughter named Mary Ann. Nick died suddenly in 1949 in Miles City. Matrona died 42 years later in April of 1991. Their son Pete died in 2011 at the age of 81 in Buffalo, Wyoming. Mary Ann died much earlier, in March of 1979.[63]

### Christ Atanasoff

Christ was born in Macedonia in 1882. He had lived and worked in Missoula for several years as a section hand on the Chicago, Milwaukee, and St. Paul Railroad lines before moving to Miles City in 1921. On August 12, 1922 he died in Miles City. He had decided to go for a swim in the Yellowstone River after eating his lunch and drowned in the rapid waters. It took several days for rescuers to recover his body. Christ had planned to bring his wife and children, who were living in Aegean Macedonia, to Miles City the next year.[64]

### Naum Atanasoff

Naum was born in Aegean Macedonia around the turn of the 20th century to parents Christ Atanasoff and Nauma Christ. He came to the U.S. at a young age and was living in Miles City by 1913. In February of 1929, Naum married Harrietta Edith Green. For most of his life in Montana, he worked as a section laborer on the railroad. He died on January 19, 1960 in Gallatin and is buried in Miles City at the Custer County Cemetery.[65]

### Dimitre Batchoff

Dimitre was born in Veles, Macedonia in 1890[66] to Alex Batchoff and Maria Nedeva[67] and immigrated to the U.S. at the age of 14.[68] Upon coming to America, Dimitre worked in the steel mills for 12 hours every day and saved enough money to attend school during the winter months, where he focused on mastering English. At 16, he left the steel mills to work for a molder in Milwaukee; but soon after that, he found employment as a lumberjack in Minnesota during the spring and summer months so he could attend school in Chicago during the winter months. At 17, he moved to Valentine, Nebraska where he dabbled in the construction business for a couple of years. Finally, in 1909, he arrived in Montana as a railroad section foreman.[69] Soon, his brother Metody joined him and by 1910, they were both living in Butte and working on the railroads.[70] But Dimitre also had other ambitions and so he found part-time work in Butte as an assistant to Burton K. Wheeler, an attorney who eventually became a Montana senator in the 1930s.[71]

Perhaps because of his experience working for an attorney, or perhaps because he understood and respected the American justice system (justice and the courts were out-of-reach for most Christians in the Ottoman Empire), Dimitre often found himself in court. For example, the financial strain felt by him and his brother rather quickly spiraled into quarrels between them. Dimitre had loaned his brother $50 in 1910, but Metody never paid him back. So, in November of 1911, Dimitre sued his brother in a Missoula County court to recover the $50.[72]

In another instance, J. D. Dobrow sued Dimitre and Milwaukee Railroad, Dimitre's employer, for $15,000 in August of 1912. Dobrow claimed that Dimitre's negligence resulted in life-altering injuries. Dimitre, who was Dobrow's superior, had ordered him to ride a handcar toward Lewistown. The ride was going well until a switch engine appeared around the bend, about one-fourth of a mile ahead. This frightened Dimitre, who pulled the brake so suddenly that Dobrow was thrown off the train. He landed on his back and injured it so severely that he was unable to work for many weeks.[73]

In May of 1913, Dimitre was asked to serve as an interpreter for a murder case near Anaconda that involved Bulgarians, Turks, Greeks and Macedonians. Dimitre was also a witness in the case, as he was present in the Greek-American Club when the victim, a Greek, was murdered. Not only did Dimitre speak English, but he also spoke Turkish and had a grasp of nearly all the Slavic languages. Thus, he was in high demand as an interpreter in Montana's courts on more than one instance.[74]

A decade later, Dimitre brought a civil suit against A. B. Melzner regarding stock ownership in a partnership firm called Cascade Silver Mines and Mills.[75] Dimitre claimed that Melzner owed him several more thousands of dollars' worth of stock when the company was sold. Melzner won the case, with the judge ruling that Dimitre had already been paid his dues.[76] Dimitre was not satisfied, however. He appealed the judgement and the original ruling was overturned: Melzner was ordered to pay Dimitre $6,000 and hand over 1,611 shares of the Silver Dyke Mining Company stock or its equivalent value in dollars.[77]

By 1920, Dimitre had settled down with his wife Sophia, who was born in Poland, and their son Boris, who was three years old at the time.[78] Before the birth of Boris, Dimitre and Sophia had a son who died in March of 1916. (He was only four months old when he died following a brief illness.)[79] Eventually, Dimitre found employment with the internal revenue department income tax division.[80]

His brother, Metody, also settled in Butte in 1912 and worked in the copper mines for two decades. He died in June of 1932 at the age of 42 due to complications from diabetes.[81] His funeral service was held at the Holy Trinity Serbian Orthodox Church in Butte with Reverend Vusich officiating.[82]

Two years later, Dimitre was appointed as the deputy U.S. Marshal for the Butte district.[83] His son Boris had left for the University of Portland a year later, in September of 1935;[84] and in March of 1937, Dimitre was appointed as chief of the law enforcement department for Montana's new liquor control board.[85] He quickly gained notoriety for his work there. In 1938, he issued a statement declaring that "Montana is now practically free of bootlegging conditions that now exist in other states." There had been 1,700 establishments clandestinely selling liquor over the bar without control prior to his reign as chief, and by October of 1938, there were only 855 establishments selling liquor and all were doing so under the proper licensure. He elaborated on his department's success: "On account of this cooperation between the state and federal forces, and due to constant vigilance, Montana today has the lowest rating of liquor crimes of any state in the union."[86]

In November of 1942, Dimitre was named acting Probation Officer for the Butte district because the previous officer abandoned his post to serve in the U.S. Army during World War II.[87] Several years later, in 1949, President Truman named Dimitre as U.S. Marshal for Montana.[88] He retired from that position four years later.[89] His son by then had settled in Portland, Oregon with his wife and two daughters, Nikili and Stefani.[90] While on a trip visiting his son in Portland in January of 1968, Dimitre had a heart attack and died.

## Christ D. Botaff

Christ was born in Aegean Macedonia in 1892. He immigrated to the U.S. in 1908 and moved to Lewistown in 1914.[91] By 1917, he was working as a farmer in Salt Creek.[92] Christ was among the first men living in Fergus County to volunteer and enlist in the U.S. military during World War I. For nearly two years he served his adoptive country, taking part in the Meuse-Argonne offensive and the Aubreville Defensive. He was honorably discharged in May of 1919.[93]

Because Christ had learned the stone mason trade from his father in Macedonia, when he returned from the war, he was earnestly employed in the construction field throughout the Western states. In 1927, he resettled in Montana, this time in Whitefish. For 17 years he worked for the Great Northern Railroad as a car helper until he retired in 1944.

Christ was also very active in his community. He served as commander of the Lion Mountain Post 276 of Veterans of Foreign Wars (VFW) in 1944. He organized and started the VFW Social Club in 1943 and managed it until 1946. He was also appointed the National Aide-de-camp of VFW in 1957 (for outstanding work as a chairman).[94] In addition to his commitments to the VFW, he supported several of Whitefish High School's sport activities; he was such a huge supporter of Whitefish sports that he received a lifetime athletic pass to high school games in 1953.[95] He even supported and coached youth baseball in the area.[96]

Christ died on January 24, 1962 in Whitefish and is buried at Whitefish Cemetery.[97] The funeral services were conducted at the Catron Chapel and he was given military honors.

## Dino Buzenoff

Dino was born on October 15, 1894 in Aegean Macedonia. By 1917 he was listed as living in Missoula and working as a laborer for the Northern Pacific Railroad Company. He served as a private for the U.S. army during World War I after enlisting in March of 1918. He was honorably discharged on December 23, 1918 as an alien enemy because "Greece [was] given as this man's residence." He moved to Great Falls in the 1920s and worked as a smelter for the rest of his life. He died on April 13, 1968 in Great Falls and is buried in the veterans' section of Highland Cemetery.[98]

## James Christoff

James was born in 1895 in Voden, Macedonia to Chris Denov and Tina Gendov and immigrated to the U.S. in 1910. He soon moved to Bowdoin and started working for the Great Northern Railway. In September of 1923, he married Alice Nelson in Kalispell. At the time of marriage, he was living in Coram and had become section foreman for the Great Northern. By 1940, the married couple was living in Belton Township and had four children: Mary K., Alice J., James W., and Marcia. In December of 1941, he accepted a position in Whitefish as road inspector and he and his family thus moved to Whitefish. James and his family were very involved and respected in their community, as one newspaper noted: "The community will miss them very much."[99]

## James Christoff

James was born in Aegean Macedonia in 1892. He immigrated to the U.S. in 1905 and immediately began working for the Northern Pacific Railroad. In 1920 he moved to Miles City, where he owned and operated the "Miles City Shone Shine Parlor" for several decades. In the 1920s, he married a young lady named Manda and their daughter, Katherine, was born in 1927. James died in January of 1958.[100]

## Theodore Christoff

Theodore, who was also known as Old Charlie, was born in Zhelevo, Macedonia in 1872. In the 1890s, he served as an officer for the Internal Macedonian Revolutionary Organization (IMRO) and moved to the United States in 1904, shortly after the suppression of the Ilinden Uprising. In Zhelevo, however, he had left behind his wife and a three-month old daughter. Theodore intended on earning enough money to bring his wife and child to America. So, that is what he began doing. He worked in Portland, Oregon for about 16 years before moving to Great Falls. For several of those years he sent money to his family, but he never heard from them. He discovered that the money he had sent had never reached them and he "blamed political mix-ups" for why his wife never received the money and why he never heard from them.

In 1958, however, he was finally reunited with his daughter, 54 years after leaving her behind. Sophia, as she was called, eventually married a man named Lucas Gadouchi at the age of 20 and immigrated to Toronto, Canada with him and her mom. It was in early 1958 that Sophia received her Canadian citizenship, which allowed her to visit Montana "to meet the father she never knew." The two spent a short but close time together, going on a tour of Glacier Park, paid for by the treasurer of S. Birch & Sons, Old Charlie's employer.

Theodore had worked at S. Birch & Sons for over 50 years since settling in Great Falls. He started as a construction worker in 1920 and he worked in that role until the age of 89. As the job became too physically demanding for him, he continued working, but "as a caretaker [that] resided on the company property doing odd chores." He was the company's caretaker until his death in November of 1971, when he died at the age of 99.

Being that he had no family in America, Charlie's co-workers were his family. At a celebration of 50 years with the company, he was asked why he was still working at the age of 99. "Good hard work keep you healthy," he replied, in his Macedonian accent. "And one nip of whiskey a day. A small one – no two." Even at his party "he kept muttering something about 'getting back to work.'" In the winter time, much of his work was spent shoveling snow, which included shoveling the snow off the grass if he had time to kill. Employees related how Theodore would often "relate some story of his youthful days in Macedonia" while emptying garbage cans and doing other chores. Well into his late 90s, he would work the vegetable garden and "spaded the plot himself." In addition to constantly working, Theodore said that eating well helped him stay healthy. In particular, he would eat "hot, spice foods he learned to like as a boy" but ensured that his diet was "not heavy on meat."

Theodore was appreciated by all for his work ethic. His story of daily life in America, as a lifelong *pechalbar*, perfectly represents the lives of many Macedonians who came to Montana. You could also say that his sense of humor represented the humor many Macedonians appreciate today just as much as they did yesterday. He notoriously joked: "I can't die; but I might go to hell."[101]

### Ilio P. Cotchoff

Ilio, who was born in Aegean Macedonia in 1890 and immigrated to America in 1909, married a Bohemian woman named Mary in the early 1910s. By 1920, the coupe was living in Fergus with their two Montana-born sons, Louis and George. Ilio worked as a farmer and his brother, Vane Cotchoff, had briefly lived with them and worked on Ilio's farm.[102]

## Alex Demitroff

Alex was born in Macedonia in 1881 and moved to Montana in the early 1900s. In 1908, he was working and living in Deer Lodge. However, that same year, he was committed to a mental institution in Warm Springs. He would only ever say his name and his birthplace, but not much more. The officials thought he had served in the military (potentially the IMRO) in the Balkans based on how he walked and his odd mannerisms. Alex wore a four-cornered piece of leather tied around his neck and would be constantly counting, one-two-three, and touching a corner of the leather while he counted. He resided in the Warm Springs Asylum until his death in June of 1946. The official cause of death was listed as dementia.[103]

## George Demitroff

George was born in a village outside of Kostur, Macedonia and came to America in 1914. For a few years he worked on the railroads near Miles City. However, he was drafted into the U.S. army during the First World War and spent several weeks overseas in the spring of 1919. He returned to Miles City in 1920 where he continued working as a section laborer on the railroads. He then moved to Butte and worked as a miner. He died in February of 1969 from heart disease and is buried at the Mountain View Cemetery in Butte.[104]

## Gust Dimitroff

In July of 1912, Gust sued Chicago, Milwaukee & Puget Sound Railroad Company to recover $45,000 in damages for injuries received while riding on a hand car. His guardian Theodore Staikos (a Greek consul in the U.S.) helped him bring the suit. The accident occurred while he was employed as a section hand on the railroad outside of Harlowton. While on a hand car, the foreman carelessly struck a cow, which resulted in Dimitroff being thrown off the car several yards. He sustained serious head and body injuries, including a fractured skull and the loss of vision in his right eye as well as damage to much of his hearing.[105] The case was removed to the U.S. federal court the following month.[106]

### John Dimitroff

John was born in Macedonia in 1894 and immigrated to the U.S. in 1912. He moved to Great Falls in 1919 and by 1930 he had moved to Cottonwood. In April of 1933 he fell gravely sick, which made him unable to work. This immobility and inability to work led to him committing suicide in his cabin in July of 1934. John is buried in Mount Olivet cemetery.[107]

### Tony Tudor Dimitroff

Tony came to the U.S. in 1910 and for several decades he was employed by the Milwaukee Railroad in Deer Lodge. He remained employed there until his retirement in 1941 and died 17 years later at the age of 69 on January 30, 1958. Reverend Basil Apostolos of the Greek Orthodox Church in Great Falls officiated the service. The only known surviving relative he had in the U.S. was Louis Stenoff, his cousin.[108]

### Alex and Clem Dimzoff

Alex was born in Ohrid, Macedonia in 1891 and moved to Montana in the early 1910s, immediately settling down in Great Falls. For much of his time in Montana he was employed by the Missoula Street Railroad Company. Alex never married and died in June of 1948. He is buried in Highland Cemetery in Great Falls. [109]

His brother Clem (also known as Clime) was also born in Ohrid one year after Alex, in 1892. He immigrated to America in 1910 and a few years later he settled in Missoula and found employment at the Missoula Street Railroad Company. In 1920, he married a woman named Lula, who was originally from

Nebraska. She had three children from a previous marriage, and together the couple had two children: Vernell and Cleo. After a work accident in 1928, in which the scaffold Clem was standing on broke and crashed to the ground, causing Clem several head and internal injuries, the family resettled in Great Falls, Clem found work there as a cement finisher for twenty years until his death in 1949. He is buried in Great Falls at Highland Cemetery.[110]

Clem and Lula had a very rough marriage. In March of 1922, after his wife made a complaint to the police, Clem was charged with intoxication and creating a disturbance at his home. He was fined $50 but did not pay it and was thus confined to jail for 25 days. He denied that he had made threats to his wife while brandishing a knife, or that he had been abusing her for some time. A decade later, in March of 1932, Lula filed an assault charge against Clem alleging that he hit her. He pleaded not guilty and the case went to trial. The matter went unresolved, but Lula filed for divorce just over a year later in August of 1933. She alleged that he hit her and swore at her often. Lula demanded an absolute divorce, meaning custody of the two children and $75 per month in alimony. Clem filed a cross-complaint denying all allegations and instead insisted that his wife treated him with cruelty by nagging him, finding fault in everything he did, and encouraging children from her prior marriage to harass, annoy and injure him. He said she repeatedly and publicly expressed in a "contemptuous manner" her total lack of affection for him. He sought sole custody of the son he fathered with her. In the end, the two shared custody and Lula was allowed $15 per month in alimony, but $25 per month if Clem was earning at least $18 per week.[111]

### Blage and Pana Eloff & Naum and Aspecia Taleff

Blage and Pana, both from Bitola, Macedonia, were married in Montana in September of 1921. However, the manner in which they came to be married to one another was not typical for Americans or Macedonians at the time. Blage (also known as Bob) first came to Chicago in 1912. He and some friends moved to Lewistown shortly after and found jobs working with the Milwaukee Railroad. The close friends he worked alongside were Newman (Naum) Taleff and Tale Zdraveff, who was Newman's father. Blage had never met them before coming to the U.S. even though they were also from Bitola. The three men moved to Great Falls and they invested in a coffee house there, where mostly Balkan men would come to talk, play cards and drink. They also sold soft drinks, candy, and tobacco at the coffee house.

In 1920, Tale returned to Macedonia and fancied the idea that Blage marry his daughter, Pana. So, Blage sent money for her passage after a year of correspondence with her and deciding that they would be a good fit. What Blage did not know until his bride was on her way to America was that Newman had done the same thing: he had been corresponding with a young woman from Bitola and she had left with Pana for the U.S. The two men waited for their brides-to-be at the Harlowton train station, and then five days later they partook in a double wedding. Pana was not too worried about the fact that she did not know Blage that well. "Sometimes you know a man 10 years and you don't know him," she later recalled.

However, after five days with her new husband, Pana had second thoughts. She had been spoiled by relatives in Macedonia throughout her whole childhood, and life with her new husband was more work than play. Pana told Blage that she wanted to go back to her family in Great Falls. Blage gave her the money for a train fare, walked her to the train and said goodbye. When Pana arrived at her brother's place, he was not happy. "I didn't stay there long. I went right back to Bob and I didn't leave him anymore. My brother said, 'You belong with your husband,' and I did." Their marriage lasted: in 1971, they celebrated their 50th wedding anniversary at the Holy Trinity

Serbian Orthodox Church.[112] The couple had three children together: Olga and Angela, twins, and James.[113]

While Blage later insisted that there was never any gambling permitted at the café he and his friends operated, the police believed otherwise. In January of 1921, police raided their Butte café and seized evidence of gambling, including a pair of dice and a dice box. There was also money in sight of the officers that had disappeared when a lookout stationed at the stairs shouted a warning, according to the police. Blage and two other men, Theo Ramas and Pete Lazanas, were arrested and each paid a $250 bond.[114] In September of 1921, the café was raided again. This time, in addition to die, eight dollars in silver were confiscated. Thirteen men were arrested and eight were held until bail was paid: Blage Eloff, Peter Cars, Louis Gois, John Tsavalos, Sam Hagi, Theodore Dimos, Mustavo Veli, and Tony Pappas.[115]

Pana worked as a dishwasher at the cafe.[116] However, the constant raids was not good for their financial well-being, so Blage returned to working for the railroad company. In 1942, he received a certificate of superior service from Milwaukee Road for completing a 12-year period without any injuries occurring to employees under his watch.[117] Blage died in 1973, and Pana then moved to Great falls to be closer to her children. She died at age 91 in March of 1995.[118]

Their son James served in World War II and had been a flight officer. He was stationed in England with the English air force and was eventually awarded the Air Medal for meritorious achievement in accomplishing aerial operations over enemy territory. As a bombardier on a B-24 Liberator bomber, he performed many missions over Germany.[119] He died in 1998 while visiting Seattle.[120]

Naum and Aspecia Taleff, the other couple that got married on the same day as Blage and Pana, had three sons and two daughters. Their son Alex, born in 1922, worked for the Great Northern for 42 years. In 1942, he enlisted in the U.S.

Army during the Second World War and served in the Persian Gulf.[121] His brother George was born in 1923. George also served in U.S. military during World War II and participated in Pacific campaigns, such as the battle for Okinawa and the liberation of Philippines. Upon returning to civilian life, George worked for Anaconda Company and was a board member of the Golden Triangle Credit Union, the Masons, the Shriners, Elks Club, and Moose Lodge.[122]

Naum and Aspecia's other son was Ted Taleff. His son, Tom, was an all-around great athlete during high school in Great Falls. He was especially known for his baseball skills. Tragically, in 1975, shortly after graduating from high school, Tom died in an auto accident with three of his friends. The community responded by establishing the Tom Taleff Sport Memorial Fund, which resulted in awarding of the Tom Taleff Award to the most inspirational player of the season.[123] The community even began a Tom Taleff Memorial Day Tournament, which is a baseball tournament held on Memorial Day weekend in Great Falls.[124]

## Daniel (Diamond) Evans

Daniel was born in the mid-1890s and immigrated to the U.S. in 1913. He first settled in Madison, Illinois, where he operated his own hat and shoe shine shop until moving to Great Falls in 1919. Daniel operated a shoe shine shop in Great Falls until his retirement in 1965 and then moved to Lewiston. He passed away in January of 1970 in Lewiston and is buried in Lewistown City Cemetery. He had never married, but he did have family in Montana, including his brother, John Gamell, who also lived in Lewistown.[125]

## John and Sultana Gamell

John and Sultana (née Liazeva) Gamell were both born in Macedonia: John in 1888 and Sultana in 1892. John was more educated than most Macedonians, as he received schooling in both Macedonia and in Germany. After returning to

Macedonia from Germany, he and Sultana married in 1906. The next year, John came to America and spent his first three years in Granite City, where he was employed at the National Tube and Foundry. John then found a job working with the railroad company and moved to South Dakota in 1910. His job kept him there for five years before it brought him to Lewistown in 1915, where he was promoted to section foreman.

He wrote for his wife and son (Louis) to come to Montana, and so they did. In the mid-1920s, the couple and their two children, Louis and John Jr. (who was born in Montana), settled in Denton, some 40 miles northwest of Lewistown. Sultana became a naturalized citizen fifteen years later in September of 1940. However, she died three years later, and a Greek Orthodox priest was summoned to officiate the burial. John, on the other hand, lived a long life. He retired from the railroad business in 1955 and lived out his life in Denton until he died in the autumn of 1980.[126]

## Nick E. Ginoff

Nick was born in 1894 to parents Evan Ginoff and Mitra Avaram and immigrated to the U.S. in 1909. He and his older brother Thomas arrived in Lincoln, Montana in the late 1910s. In November, Nick enlisted in the U.S. military but was shortly thereafter honorably discharged. Thomas died shortly after at the age of 37 in November of 1924. His other brother, Pete, then came to Montana the next year and the two worked as farmers together. In the late 1930s, Nick married Mable (who was originally from Wisconsin) in Missoula. They soon after settled in Helmville where Nick continued to work as a rancher. He filed a petition for the nomination to office of county commissioner in Butte in June of 1938 under the Republican ticket. In the 1950s, he served as the representative of the Missoula Electric Cooperative and on the boosters for the Blackfoot Telephone Cooperative. Nick died in Missoula in August of 1961.[127]

## Peter E. Ginoff

Peter, brother to Nick Ginoff above, was born in 1896 and came to the U.S. in 1925. He operated a farm near Missoula for most of his life. His specialty was poultry. By the late 1940s, he operated a 267-acre farm, with 600 turkeys. Peter was a dedicated farmer: he often slept in a tent near the turkey pen and set up owl traps on the ends of high poles and did his best to protect the flock from predators. He had no outside help on his farm, but his wife (Marie, from Hungary) played a crucial role in the farm's operations. In addition to the large turkey flock, the farm had 70 geese, 500 fryer chickens, 150 laying hens, 44 pigs, 55 whiteface cattle, 30 acres of hay and 140 acres in wheat, barley, oats and peas. He and his wife had two children: Peter Jr. and Connie. Peter Sr. had also been employed at Olney Motors and Wakeley Dodge in Missoula. He was a committed member of the Missoula Elks Lodge and the Missoula Senior Citizens organization.[128]

## Nurmi George

Nurmi came to America in 1906 and very soon found himself in Butte. Around 1920 he resettled in Hamilton and worked as a gardener for J. O. Read. He was well known in Hamilton and Missoula, especially in the Macedonian and Balkan community. On New Year's Day of 1941, he fell gravely ill. He had complained at breakfast that he felt sick and asked Matt Koch, in whose cabin he was staying near Corvallis, to come back in a little bit to take him to a hospital if he felt worse. When Koch came to the cabin, Nurmi did not respond and was discovered dead in the bedroom. At his funeral, his countrymen were his pallbearers: George Regins, Marion Mincoff, Pete Shungaris, George Paulos, Alec Evanoff, and William Dimitroff. Nurmi is buried in Riverview Cemetery.[129]

## Van Janoff

Van Janoff (also known as Van Janeff) was born in Kostur, Macedonia in 1897 to parents Nicholas Janov and Theodosia Kolarov and immigrated to America in 1908. Within a decade he had moved to Butte and started working in the copper mines. In 1927 he married Irene, a native of Montana. By 1940, the couple was living in Butte. Van died on April 5, 1973 from a brain injury he had sustained a few weeks prior. His funeral services were conducted by Reverend Jovan Kovacevich of Butte's Serbian Orthodox Church. Van is buried at Mountain View Cemetery in Butte.[130]

## John Kostoff

John Kostoff was born in Aegean Macedonia and came to America in the 1910s. For 20 years he worked as a miner in Butte until his death on January 15, 1936, which was due to a mining accident. Survivors included two sisters in Macedonia and a cousin, Elia Damaskey, who was living in Butte.[131]

## Louis Kostoff

Louis was born in Macedonia on March 8, 1890. At the age of 21 he immigrated to the U.S. and first settled in Kansas City. For several years he then labored on the railroads in North Dakota before moving to Deer Lodge in the late 1920s. In 1930, he was an inmate at the Deer Lodge Prison (for an unspecified crime). Once he was released from prison, he found employment at the Milwaukee Road Shops until his retirement in 1955. He had a wife named Marian and three children. Louis died on February 3, 1960 and is buried at Hillcrest Cemetery.[132]

## John and Mary Kosty

John was born in eastern Macedonia in 1885 and immigrated to the U.S. in 1909, a few months after marrying Mary, who was one year his younger. Three years later, Mary and their son, Christopher, followed John to America, and they settled in Miles City. In addition to Christopher, the

Macedonian-born couple had four other kids: Kathryn, Emma, Victor, and Eva. John worked as a gardener in Miles City and died suddenly on November 11, 1925. Mary died several decades later in 1970.[133]

## Alexander Ladinoff

Alexander Ladinoff, born in 1888, immigrated to the U.S. in 1910. He first settled in Detroit, but after a few years traversed across the Midwest and found work in South Dakota. There, he married Bertha Earls in April of 1917 and shortly thereafter moved to Chouteau County in Montana and began working for the Great Northern as a machinist. In 1924, the couple permanently settled in Whitefish. They had five children together: Boris, Sulen, Flora, Hazel, and Abel. Alexander died in November of 1952 and his wife in July of 1966. They are buried at the Whitefish Cemetery.[134]

Their son Boris followed in his dad's footsteps. In February of 1940, he accepted a job offer from the Great Northern as a mechanic. Four years later, however, he enlisted in the U.S. military and participated in the Rhineland campaign overseas during the Second World War. For his service, he was awarded the good conduct medal, European-African-Middle Eastern theater service medal, and the army of occupation of Germany medal; Boris was honorably discharged in June of 1946. His brother, Alex Jr., entered military service just a few months after him and was awarded the Asiatic-Pacific service medal, meritorious unit award, army of occupation medal for Japan, victor medal, and the good conduct medal.

Boris was a very patriotic American. In February of 1951, he was commander of the Bear Paw post of the VFW in Havre and, as the group's leader, offered Bear Paw's services to protect Havre citizens in case of a future enemy attack on Montana. He wrote a letter to Mayor Oval Hatler stating that, by unanimous vote, the group was volunteering their services to form civil defense plans for the community's protection. In his letter, Boris wrote: "As men who have faced the enemy in combat and have witnessed at first hand destruction of war and the resulting chaos and suffering, we feel our experience and training should be utilized in any program or plans to defend the community from attack or to soften the blow should it fall."

In November of 1968, Richard W. Homan, commander in chief of the national VFW organization, appointed Boris as a national aide-de-camp of VFW for his commitment and service. He said of Boris: "The continued success of our organization depends on the foundation we have built with qualified and dedicated leadership, such as that shown by Mr. Lodinoff. I know I can count on a job well done whenever he is called upon to serve the Veterans of Foreign Wars." Boris died in December of 2002 at age 83.[135]

## Nick Lazoff

Nick was born in 1895 and moved to the U.S. in the 1910s. In 1934, he married a woman named Stella. Together they had one son named Lawrence, and by 1940, the family was living in Kircher. For most of his life in Montana, Nick worked as a farmer. He died on August 21, 1972. His son Lawrence married Lavonne Smith in 1964 and the coupe settled in Billings in 1966. For three decades, Lawrence worked at Midland-Materials as a mechanic and a welder. He was an avid hunter and fisher, as well as a member of the National Rifle Association and the Yellowstone Rifle Club. Lawrence died in February of 1997 at the age of 60.[136]

## Louis Luchis

Louis was born in Aegean Macedonia in 1893 and immigrated to the U.S. in 1912, immediately settling in Butte. For four decades he worked in the copper mines until his retirement in 1952. He married Caroline, from Montana, but the two did not have any children. Caroline died in 1958 and Louis died eight years later in April of 1966. His brothers, nephews and nieces residing in Macedonia were his only survivors. The Serbian priest, Dositei Obradovich, officiated his funeral service.[137]

### George Makedonski

In the summer of 1910, a trial was held in Butte in which George Makedonski sued the Oregon Short Line Railroad. He claimed that, in November of 1909, he had bought a ticket from the company to travel from Butte to Armstead. In his possession he had a trunk that the company undertook to carry for him. The company lost the trunk and George claimed it contained articles worth $290. George originally was granted $150 for the articles by the court of Justice Egan. However, the company appealed that decision and the case was sent to Judge Lynch's court.[138] George could not speak English, so he needed a Macedonian interpreter.[139] The trial lasted three days and George was awarded a final verdict of $77.[140]

### Theodore Mano

Theodore was born in Aegean Macedonia in 1888.[141] He arrived in Butte in 1924 and worked in the copper mines until his death following a long illness in September of 1949. There were no known survivors in the U.S.[142]

### Paul and Donna Mike

Paul was born in 1888 in Lerin, Macedonia and came to America in 1908. He bounced around many places in Montana, from Yellowstone to Broadview to Hobson. He worked as a section foreman on the railroad and he and his wife Donna (née Eftoff) had five children: Katherine, Helen, Margaret, Christ and Ruth. Paul died on April 13, 1968, less than a year after Donna died. Their first-born, Katherine, was born in Macedonia in 1910. In 1930, Katherine married William K. Shamanoff, also born in Macedonia. The marriage took place in Great Falls. William's parents were Christ Shamanoff and Mary Tanoff. The couple moved to Bozeman in the 1930s and had two children: Mary and Patricia. Together, they owned a restaurant where William worked as the cook and Katherine as a waitress. William died on July 6, 1964 in Billings. Katherine died many years later in October of 2000, and they are buried together at Mountainview Cemetery.[143]

The name of the restaurant that William and Katherine operated was called Bill's Grill. Their daughters, Patty and Mary, would wash dishes and peel potatoes for the restaurant. In 1947, the family moved from Bozeman to Billings. Patty graduated from Billings Senior High in 1952 and immediately began work as an executive secretary at George L. Tracy's firm. She married F. Duane Rowley in 1955 and moved to Missoula while Duane studied at the University of Missoula and Patty worked for the city manager as an executive secretary. The couple moved back to Billings and had three children together. In 1962, they resettled in Missoula and opened different businesses, including a door sales shop and Rowley Construction (in Lolo). The couple retired in 1983 and moved to Flathead Lake. Patty was very involved in her community and was a member of the Christian Women of Polson Organization, Polson Booster Club, American Lighting Association, Flathead Lakers, Polson Chamber of Commerce, Polson Community Development, and Flathead Builders Association.[144]

## Lazar Nanoff

Lazar was born in Lerin, Macedonia in 1887. He came to the U.S. in the early 1910s, and by the mid-1910s he was working as a farmer in Wakpala, South Dakota. He was drafted into the U.S. army during World War I and served as a private for a year. In the mid-1920s, Lazar got married and had a son named Lawrence, who was born in 1927. Shortly after, the family moved to Poplar and then Frazer, where Lazar continued to farm until his death in April of 1953.[145]

## Naso Naumoff

Naso was born in Aegean Macedonia 1893. By 1917 he was living in Cobury and working on the Great Northern.[146] In 1932, he sued the railway company for $14,000 due to injuries he sustained while working in Butte.[147] His injuries came from an accident that involved a motor car and a push car used in section work. Naso insisted he was permanently disabled and unable to work, and that his condition would only get worse. The defendant said that there was insufficient evidence that the company was negligent or liable. The case was likely settled outside of the court system.[148]

## George and Dina Nickoloff

George was born in Dumbeni (Aegean Macedonia) in 1893. At the age of 10, he moved to Athens, Greece, where he worked for "three francs a day." Several years later, in 1909, he immigrated to Illinois. Like many Macedonians, he first found work in Granite City, where he lived with friends and family members. His first job was with the American Glass Factory in Alton, just outside of Granite City. In 1910 he landed a job with a gang on the Milwaukee Railroad, but he was laid off in December 1910; so, he went back to Granite City and found a job with the American Car Foundry in Madison. However, he did not give up on his dream to work on the railroads and in the spring of 1911, he found a job with Northern Pacific in Minnesota, which took him through several cities and states over the next few years: Trenton, North Dakota; Superior, Wisconsin; Tampico, Montana; and Lanark, Montana. In Lanark in 1913, he was promoted to section foreman and was transferred to Brockton in June of 1914. He worked in Brockton as a foreman until his retirement in 1958, where after he moved to Culbertson.

As a foreman, George never fired anyone. He worked hard and expected the same from his subordinates; because he led by example, his gang was devoted to him. He was also admired for his courage. One time, George had left his house in the late 1920s and was halfway uptown when he saw a coal car shoot out of an old-style coal chute. He ran to the tool house, put the motor car on the rails, and chased the coal car for three miles until he caught up to it; he climbed on top of it in order to stop it, and grabbed the flag to signal a passenger train ahead. He averted a potential disaster, as the passenger train was headed in the direction of the runaway coal car but could not see it as it was on a bend.

In 1929, George broke his leg on the job and was given a long leave of absence. So, he traveled back to Macedonia and married to Dina, who was 22 years old at the time. Dina described how they met: "He saw me walking in a field barefoot and sat at the side of the field and watched me work. He didn't say anything and I didn't either. Things were different in those days. I knew his sister and she introduced us and we became engaged." Like most Macedonian weddings, their wedding lasted three days.

In Montana, the happy couple had five children: Nickola, John, James, Elia and Christine. George died in April of 1969. Nine years later, in September of 1978, Dina finally got her citizenship papers after 48 years in America. She had taken the test twice beforevbut was so nervous both times that she was unable to answer the questions. Dina died in 1993 in Billings.[149]

Their son John, at the age of 21, was promoted to corporal in November of 1953 while serving in the 45th infantry division in Korea. He had been in Korea since December of 1951.[150] Their other son, Elia, received his doctorate in Rehabilitation from the University of Arizona in October of 1975.[151] In May of 1985, he was honored with an award by the scholarship foundation of Eastern Montana College as a distinguished professor. He was especially noted for his work in deaf education.[152]

## Louis Phillips

Louis was born in Aegean Macedonia in the late 1880s to Phillip Zisov and Mitra Christof. His immigration date is unknown, but by 1917 he was living in Valier, Montana. In July of 1918, Louis was inducted into the U.S. military and served until he was honorably discharged in December of that same year. He came back to Valier and continued working for the railroad company. Very shortly afterwards, in 1919, he married Blanche Ruth of Wisconsin and the couple went on to have seven children: Clifford, Louise, Edward, Lyle, Emmett, Thomas and Roger. Clifford died in 1939. Louis died on December 12, 1958 and is buried at Lakeview Cemetery in Valier. His wife died 36 years later in 1994.[153]

## Vane Phillips

Vane Phillips was born in Macedonia in 1886. He came to America in 1906, first settling in St. Louis. In 1914, he moved to Winnett, Montana. He died in September of 1961 in Lewistown and is buried in the Winnett Cemetery. His funeral service was held at First Lutheran Church, with Reverend David Zietlow officiating.[154]

## Pasku Popeka (Popescu)

Pasku was born in Macedonia in 1888 and immigrated to the United States in 1907. In 1920, he was living in Plentywood and working as a prep in a restaurant.[155] In 1927, he married Josephine Westering, who died in 1934. The couple had two children before she died, Gene and James. Around the same time, Pasku and his brother Tache James started a restaurant together. Pasku retired in 1959 and remained in Plentywood for the rest of his life, when he killed himself at the age of 77 in in March of 1965. The reverend at Plentywood Lutheran Church conducted his funeral services and Pasku was buried with military honors at Plentywood Cemetery.[156]

## Tache Jim Popescu

Tache was born in Macedonia in the late 19th century. He was a teacher there for four years but escaped Macedonia when the Balkan Wars broke out. He arrived in the U.S. in 1913 and found work as a cook and dishwasher in New York City and shortly thereafter found his way to his brother in Iowa City, Iowa. In 1916, Tache and his brother moved to Plentywood and eventually opened Elgin Cafe. His brother died first, and then Tache died on March 18, 1973, unmarried and childless.[157]

## George Regins

George was born in 1891 in Aegean Macedonia to parents Constantine Redjion and Techa Mastera. He came to America in 1912 and settled in Hamilton, Montana, and over a decade later he married Bessie Wright in September of 1925. For most of his Montanan life, he worked as a farmer. Bessie died in 1949, and over a year later, on October 7, 1950, George remarried to Genevieve Iten. He died in 1981 and is buried at the Riverview Cemetery in Hamilton.[158]

## John and Naumka Ristoff

John, who also went by Jovantche, was born in 1882 and Naumka (née Zdraveva) was born the year before. The couple married in Bitola in 1904, and in 1911, their son Louie was born; in that same year, John ventured to America, and in 1914 he came to Miles City, where he first worked on the railroads and then opened a shoe shine shop. In 1921, Naumka and Louie joined John and they went on to have two more sons, Jimmy and Alek, and a daughter named Florence. They settled near Miles City in Custer County and John left the shoe shine business for farming. The family farm was known locally as Pirogue Island. Their daughter Florence, who was born in 1925, died from a prolonged illness is October of 1930. Naumka died in October of 1963 and John passed away in September of 1967. They are buried at the Custer County Cemetery in Miles City.

Their son Jimmy, who was born in 1922, served in the U.S. military during World War II. He served in the Asiatic Pacific Theater and in Luzon with the Akita Military Government Team. Jimmy received a Good Conduct Medal, Asiatic Pacific Medal, Army of Occupation Medal (for Japan), Philippine Liberation Medal, and one Bronze Star and Victory Medal. He was honorably discharged from service on November 13, 1946.[159]

## Norman S. Shotnokoff

Norman was born in 1893 and came to America in the 1910s. He bounced around several states before he met a young woman named Clarise in Wisconsin. The two soon got married. In the 1930s they moved to Brockton with their three children: Norman, Phyllis, and Margaret. In 1940, Norman was listed as working as a barber at a barber shop while his son, Norman, Jr. (20 at the time), was working as a waiter.[160] Three years later, however, Norman, Jr. died while serving in the military overseas during World War II.[161] He left behind a young wife that he had married just over a year before shipping off to Europe.[162] Norman Sr. moved to Portland, Oregon shortly afterwards and died in April of 1967.[163]

## Chris Sotir

Chris was born in Veria, Macedonia in 1892 and immigrated to America in 1910. He shortly thereafter arrived in Butte, where he would remain for the rest of his life, working both as a farmer and a copper miner. Chris enlisted in the U.S. military during World War I and served for his country from May of 1918 to February of 1919. He died in July of 1961 in Butte.[164]

## Nick Spiroff

Nick Spiroff was born in Aegean Macedonia in 1891 and immigrated to the U.S. in 1907. He was living in Fergus in 1920 with his Austrian born wife, Anna, and two Montana-born kids, Nick Jr. and Katherine. His occupation was a farmer.[165]

## Louie Stenoff

Louie was born in Macedonia in a village outside of Kostur in 1896. He arrived in America in 1913 and immediately rode out to Montana, where he would spend several decades working in restaurants and mines in Butte. He knew several Macedonians there, including his cousin, Tudor Dimitroff. In the early 1950s, he moved to Rock Springs, Wyoming and worked in the coal mines there. By 1955 he was getting too old for mining work, so he moved to Lava Hot Springs, Idaho and worked as the head gardener for the Lava Foundation until 1964. Like many Macedonians who traveled out West, he never married.[166] He died in Idaho on July 15, 1980, at the age of 83, and is buried at Mountain View Cemetery in Pocatello, Idaho.[167]

Although he died in Idaho, Louie spent much of his life in Montana. He remained close with many Macedonians, which was generally a good thing; but in some instances, it caused problems. In May of 1922, Louie took Apostal Miofsky to court, accusing Miofsky of beating him up in April of 1922. Louie insisted that he was minding his own business when Miofsky struck him on the head with a hammer, causing him permanent injuries and to miss several weeks of work,[168] and thus demanded $3,000 in damages.[169] The news reported that the entire Balkan "colony of Deer Lodge was present." Miofsky was fined $20 for the assault.[170] However, in November of 1922 the case was appealed and went to trial by jury in Powell County, after Miofsky requested that the trial be held there. The court now brought in two different interpreters, as the men claimed to be from different provinces of Macedonia and could not understand each other's dialect. During this second go-around, the jury found in favor of Miofsky.[171]

Nearly three decades later, in the spring of 1950, Louie sued P. V. Dimitroff for back wages and the judge decided the case should be decided by a jury. Louie claimed that Dimitroff owed him the money for labor he performed for him during 1949. Dimitroff had hired Louie in July of 1949 to work as a truckman for him, loading and hauling produce from his farm to various western Montana markets. Louie was never paid for the work. The jury awarded the full amount asked, which was $1,005. The jury only deliberated for thirty minutes.[172]

## Christo and Steve Tanaskoff

Christo was born in Aegean Macedonia in 1887 and immigrated to the U.S. in 1906 with his wife Pano. The two were married in Macedonia in 1904. In the early 1910s, the two moved to Fergus County in Montana, but Pano was not happy there. Thus, in November of 1915, she left him and Christo filed for a divorce from her on the ground of desertion. The divorce was granted in April of 1916. By 1930, Christo had moved to Lewis and Clark County, where he was working as a farm hand at a dairy ranch. During his stay in Montana, he found himself in trouble with the law on more than one occasion. In March of 1925, he served 40 days in jail and paid a $50 fine for violating the national prohibition on alcohol. He was also arrested and fined in 1935 for driving without the proper license.[173]

His brother Steve, who was also living in Montana, found himself in deeper trouble with the law. In April of 1923, Steve was charged with a misdemeanor for selling morphine and cocaine. He pleaded not guilty and his bond was fixed at $1,500.[174] In late April, the case went before trial in front of Judge Lynch.[175] There, Steve reversed his plea and stated he was guilty. The judge sentenced him to two years in state prison and ordered him to pay a fine of $500.[176] While he was not convicted of selling narcotics, Steve was convicted for possessing morphine. In December of that same year, Attorney General W. D. Rankin proclaimed that Tanaskoff was entitled to release because the state law under which Tanaskoff had been sentenced was held invalid by the state supreme court. The prison sentence and fine were valid, but not the sentence that required Tanaskoff to serve one day in prison for each $2 of the fine that he could not afford to pay. Judge Lynch set aside the sentence and released Steve on December 23.[177] Several years later Steve was back in the justice system, this time charged with grand larceny for stealing a Jersey cow in the autumn of 1936.[178]

Steve was born in 1887 and eventually settled down in Butte in 1940, where he worked as a metal miner.[179] Before that he had worked different farming jobs throughout Montana.[180]

## Chris and Dena Tarpo

Chris was born in 1890 and immigrated to the U.S. in 1909. He traveled back to Macedonia and married Dena, from his village, and she came back with him to Montana in 1921. As soon as she joined Chris in Harlowton, they began having kids: Chris, Louis, William, and Lena. Chris (Sr.) worked as a section foreman for the railroad company.[181]

## Nick Thompson

Nick was born in Macedonia around 1890 and came to the U.S. in 1908. He went straight to Montana. For several years he worked on the railroads in Teton County, eventually achieving section foreman status. However, being a section foreman was not fulfilling enough. Using some of the money he earned, he enrolled in the Coyne Electrical School in Chicago.

After learning all he needed to know about electricity and engineering, he moved back to Montana, this time settling in Great Falls. He did not, however, return to working on the railroads. His education and time in Chicago provided him with the motivation and knowhow to dabble in the movie business, and he would soon became known as a pioneer of the motion picture industry in Montana. In November of 1928, he rigged his truck with the necessary equipment that he had acquired in Chicago and showed his first movie in Coffee Creek. He then started traveling around Great Falls and Helena showing movies out of his truck. With his success came more money, and he opened and operated movie theaters throughout Montana, including in Denton, Coffee Creek, Harlowton, Sun River, and Great Falls.

In the late 1930s, his nephew, George Kuzoff, came to Great Falls and lived with him for a few years. But shortly after George left, Nick died in Great Falls on November 6, 1946. When he died, he left a $15,000 estate, which consisted mostly of machinery and equipment. He had no heirs in the U.S., but his heirs were listed as a sister and brother in Macedonia.[182]

### James (John) Tricoff

James was born in Bitola, Macedonia in 1894.[183] He immigrated to the U.S. in his late teenage years and almost immediately settled in Butte to work in the mines.[184] Yet, he soon found himself in trouble with the law. Unlike many of his compatriots, he had no desire to serve as an American soldier. Thus, in January of 1918, he was arrested by Butte Police Captain Mike O'Donnell on charges of desertion for failing to report for examination under the draft. A notice card had been mailed to him and he had refused to fill it out.[185] Over the next two decades he experienced some hard times, especially during the Great Depression. For example, in March of 1938 the Silver Bow County Commissioners gave him $16 as "aid to the poor."[186]

By 1940, he was still living in Butte. James had never married and had now transitioned into farming.[187] He lived and worked as a rancher in Butte until his retirement in 1960 and then moved to Beaverhead County. He passed away at the age of 81, in October of 1975, at the Parkview Acres Nursing Home in Dillon. He had no known survivors in the U.S.[188] He is buried at Mountain View Cemetery in Dillon.[189]

## Mike Ulani

Mike Ulani was born in 1884 in Aegean Macedonia and immigrated to the U.S. in 1916. He jumped around the country before settling down in Butte in the 1930s. Throughout his entire time in the U.S., he remained unmarried and was eventually plagued with depression. Mike committed suicide in November of 1956. His funeral was officiated by the Holy Trinity Serbian Orthodox Church's priest, Mileta Simonovich, and his burial was at Sunset Memorial Gardens just outside of Butte. Fellow Macedonian, Louie Stenoff, was a pallbearer at his funeral.[190]

## James P. Vasileff

James was born on November 25, 1896 in Voden, Macedonia. In 1918 he moved to Mining City where he worked as a section foreman for the railroad company. He married Katie Hill in 1937. Katie died in 1980 and James died in May of 1982. The Serbian Orthodox priest, Petar Milosevich, officiated his service. The only known surviving relative of James was his sister, Theodora Jondy, who was living in Voden at the time.[191]

## Mary Yankoff

Mary was born in Macedonia in 1882 and came to the U.S. in 1911, immediately settling in Miles City. Her husband passed away shortly after their arrival and she was left with their son, Louis. In the late 1920s, she was working as a house helper for a private family and was recorded as living with two Yugoslavians in Miles City, Theodore Wassel and Anthony George. At the time of her death in Miles City in March of 1951, her son Louis was overseas serving in the Korean War. Her daughter was married to Oswald Gaub. Mary had five grandchildren.[192]

# 3
# List of Macedonians in Montana

The following table is a list of 645 Macedonians that worked and lived in Montana for a period of time. The individual's first name, surname, birth year, and primary residence in Montana are provided. This information has been collected and compiled by searching through U.S. Census data, from 1910 to 1940; World War I Draft Registration Cards; Military Service documents; marriage licenses; birth and death certificates; and newspaper articles.

| First Name | Surname | Year Born | Montana Residence |
|---|---|---|---|
| Paulo | Adgiorsky | 1892 | Lombard |
| Vasil | Agiorsky | 1900 | Rosebud |
| Glegor | Alanaff | N/A | Dawson |
| Naum | Alantesoff | N/A | Dawson |
| Vasil | Aleexoff | N/A | Billings |
| Mike | Alenkoff | 1888 | Big Porcupine |
| Petro | Alhansoff | 1882 | Bowdoin |
| Thene | Anastaiff | N/A | Dawson |
| Nick | Anastasoff | 1890 | Poplar |
| Arso | Anastass | 1881 | Cottonwood |
| Vasil | Andanoff | 1878 | Rosebud |
| Nick | Andanoff | 1893 | Rosebud |
| Frederick | Andersy | 1879 | Superior |
| Karati | Andonoff | 1895 | Treasure |
| Steve | Angelo | 1887 | Corbin |
| Vasie | Angeloff | 1870 | Fergus |
| Christ | Angeloff | 1883 | Yellowstone |
| Peter | Angeloff | 1885 | Yellowstone |
| Nicola | Angeloff | 1895 | Deer Lodge |
| Nick | Angeloff | 1897 | Miles City |

| | | | |
|---|---|---|---|
| Matrona Makedonski | Angeloff | 1901 | Miles City |
| Nick | Angeloff | 1895 | Miles City |
| Lee | Angeloff | 1904 | Hedgesville |
| Anna | Angeloff | N/A | Hedgesville |
| Jordon | Angeloff | 1885 | Powell |
| Tody | Angeoff | 1876 | Meagher |
| Angelo | Angilofsky | 1896 | Great Falls |
| Cristo | Antenosoff | 1884 | Fergus |
| Jerogr | Antonoff | 1890 | Lombard |
| Louis | Apastalof | N/A | Dawson |
| Todor | Apostoloff | 1892 | Elk Park |
| Jacob | Appostol | 1864 | Armington |
| Petro | Arger | N/A | Dawson |
| Leonida | Argiroff | 1885 | Lombard |
| Lozio | Atanasoff | 1890 | Miles City |
| Nums | Atanasoff | 1881 | Rosebud |
| Nikala | Atanasoff | 1888 | Missoula |
| Nicola | Atanasoff | 1872 | Car |
| Naum | Atanasoff | 1900 | Miles City |
| Christ | Atanasoff | 1882 | Missoula |
| George | Atanasoff | 1892 | Warland |
| Eane | Atanasoff | 1899 | Warland |
| Karsto | Auknloff | 1882 | Rosebud |
| Dimotro | Bachiff | 1875 | Warland |
| Nick | Badanoheff | 1887 | Lombard |
| George | Bakaloff | 1886 | St. Ignatius |
| George | Baliff | 1886 | Armington |
| Savandy | Bancheff | 1890 | Fergus |
| Dimitre | Batchoff | 1890 | Butte |
| Metody | Batchoff | 1890 | Butte |
| Vancho | Bechkaroff | 1862 | Butte |
| Crist | Betro | 1889 | Meagher |
| Dine | Bidjoff | 1885 | Phillips |
| Jim | Bill | 1883 | Fergus |

| | | | |
|---|---|---|---|
| Nick | Bill | 1884 | Fergus |
| Crist | Bill | 1885 | Fergus |
| John V. | Bitseff | 1897 | Plains |
| F | Blaxeff | 1872 | Box Elder |
| Lewis | Blaxeff | 1889 | Box Elder |
| Nasto | Blogeff | 1886 | Armington |
| Christ D. | Botaff | 1892 | Whitefish |
| Dims | Bozinoff | 1890 | Chinook |
| Gligor | Bozinoff | 1881 | St. Regis |
| Tom | Busensky | 1884 | Warland |
| Din | Buzenoff | 1894 | Missoula |
| Jeorge | Cadniakoff | 1870 | Lombard |
| Vasel | Canolantenoff | N/A | Dawson |
| Tony | Charleff | 1870 | Warland |
| Starno | Choleff | 1865 | Corbin |
| Gust | Chreest | N/A | Helena |
| Paul | Chris | 1877 | Havre |
| Steef | Chris | 1890 | Lombard |
| Tom | Christ | 1880 | Silver Bow |
| Nick | Christ | N/A | Dawson |
| Ted | Christ | 1895 | Cascade |
| Paul | Christ | 1869 | Charlo |
| Peter | Christ | 1875 | Charlo |
| Steve | Christ | 1888 | Miles City |
| Traun | Christiloff | 1870 | Yellowstone |
| Vincetre | Christo | N/A | Dawson |
| Demetre | Christof | N/A | Dawson |
| Mike | Christoff | 1882 | Missoula |
| Demitri | Christoff | 1873 | Superior |
| Sam | Christoff | 1887 | Lewis and Clark |
| Nicola | Christoff | 1881 | Missoula |
| Jane | Christoff | 1891 | Miles City |
| Paul | Christoff | 1885 | Whitefish |
| Nick | Christoff | 1893 | Bowdoin |
| Demetri | Christoff | 1882 | Mineral |

| | | | |
|---|---|---|---|
| George | Christoff | 1875 | Roosevelt |
| Peter | Christoff | 1893 | Bowdoin |
| Svatco | Christoff | 1888 | Cascade |
| James | Christoff | 1895 | Belton |
| Lazo | Christoff | 1893 | Choteau |
| George | Christoff | 1890 | Great Falls |
| Vasil | Christoff | 1874 | Butte |
| George | Christoff | 1898 | Butte |
| Nicholas | Christoff | 1889 | Chinook |
| Georgi | Christoff | 1887 | Fergus |
| Marko | Christoff | 1882 | Hill |
| Vane | Christoff | 1898 | Fergus |
| Mannis | Christoff | 1899 | Bowdoin |
| Torjean | Christoff | 1868 | Lombard |
| Jim | Christoff | 1870 | Lombard |
| Toshi | Christoff | 1875 | Lombard |
| Jrorgr | Christoff | 1881 | Lombard |
| James | Christoff | 1892 | Miles City |
| Dimetri | Christoff | 1888 | Chinook |
| Kiro | Christoff | 1891 | Elk Park |
| Theodore | Christoff | 1872 | Great Falls |
| George | Claristoff | 1884 | Livingston |
| Slavic | Clemhoff | 1890 | Armington |
| Nicolo | Costoff | 1872 | Meagher |
| Ilio P. | Cotchoff | 1890 | Fergus |
| Tom | Crist | 1882 | Meagher |
| Tom | Custoff | 1894 | Malta |
| John | Dakoff | 1886 | Lombard |
| Georgi | Daliseff | 1888 | Fergus |
| Vasil | Daloff | 1883 | Warland |
| Thomas | Danl | 1893 | Deer Lodge |
| Louis | Danoff | N/A | Dawson |
| Nickola | Dashaff | N/A | Dawson |
| Vasil | Daskaloff | 1875 | Lombard |
| Tuchi | Daskaloff | 1880 | Lombard |

| | | | |
|---|---|---|---|
| Demetry | Degaloff | 1871 | Rosebud |
| George | Delchiff | 1873 | Warland |
| Slamco | Deloff | 1888 | Butte |
| John | Demeatre | 1890 | Armington |
| Lalir | Demehoref | N/A | Dawson |
| Apostol | Demetre | N/A | Dawson |
| George | Demetroff | 1881 | Rosebud |
| Vangel | Demetroff | 1882 | Rosebud |
| Paudro | Demetroff | 1880 | Rosebud |
| Vargo | Demetroff | N/A | Dawson |
| Arger | Demetroff | N/A | Dawson |
| Alex | Demitroff | 1881 | Warm Springs |
| George | Demitroff | 1892 | Miles City |
| Gorge | Demitroff | 1886 | Lombard |
| Tom | Demoff | 1895 | Libby |
| George | Demoff | 1893 | Libby |
| Costo | Demstroff | 1883 | Warland |
| Dimibro | Deneda | 1883 | Warland |
| Christo | Denoff | N/A | Dawson |
| Dane | Denskeff | N/A | Dawson |
| Pete | Dichoff | 1880 | Butte |
| Lavzo | Dimatroff | 1863 | Wolf Point |
| Nick | Dimetroff | 1888 | Chinook |
| Kosta | Dimetrose | 1882 | Butte |
| Pat | Dimieff | 1870 | Bearmouth |
| Alex | Dimintroff | 1890 | Missoula |
| Labro | Dimistroff | 1892 | Lombard |
| Kosta | Dimitri | 1891 | Lombard |
| Gust | Dimitroff | N/A | N/A |
| Alexander | Dimitroff | 1889 | Missoula |
| John | Dimitroff | 1884 | Butte |
| Thomas | Dimitroff | 1881 | Fergus |
| Tony | Dimitroff | 1886 | Deer Lodge |
| Nako | Dimitroff | 1899 | Deer Lodge |
| John | Dimitroff | 1899 | Butte |

| | | | |
|---|---|---|---|
| John | Dimitroff | 1894 | Cottonwood |
| Ilijo | Dimitroff | 1888 | Lombard |
| John | Dimitroff | 1880 | Missoula |
| George | Dimoff | 1889 | Cascade |
| Petsovch | Dimoff | 1883 | Cottonwood |
| Don | Dimoff | 1893 | Libby |
| Chris | Dimoff | 1884 | Lombard |
| Masco | Dimoff | 1894 | Warland |
| Torpo | Dimoff | 1888 | Yellowstone |
| Clem (Clime) | Dimzoff | 1892 | Great Falls |
| Alex | Dimzoff | 1891 | Missoula |
| Dimetry | Dineff | 1879 | Park |
| Lazo G. | Dineff | 1882 | Havre |
| Louis | Dineff | 1884 | Great Falls |
| Jeregr | Dineff | 1875 | Lombard |
| Tachi | Dineff | 1892 | Lombard |
| Nick | Dineff | 1874 | Prarie |
| Labro | Dineff | 1869 | Warland |
| Nick | Dinoff | 1862 | Great Falls |
| Nick | Dinoff | 1877 | Miles City |
| Pete | Dirmo | 1892 | Bearmouth |
| Tony | Domitroff | 1886 | Charlo |
| Chroste | Doneff | 1877 | Armington |
| Tom | Doot | 1893 | Charlo |
| Chris | Doumoff | 1873 | Lombard |
| Jim | Drigiroff | 1889 | Cottonwood |
| Franc | Ducleff | 1890 | Bearmouth |
| George | Duroff | 1894 | Deer Lodge |
| Christ | Eftinoff | 1891 | Miles City |
| Christ | Eftinoff | 1879 | Miles City |
| Pando | Eliaff | 1867 | Rosebud |
| Christ | Elieff | 1894 | Libby |
| Metody | Elieff | 1894 | Neihart |
| Atanas | Elieff | 1900 | Ferus |
| Blage | Eloff | 1893 | Superior |

| | | | |
|---|---|---|---|
| Para | Eloff (Taleff) | N/A | Superior |
| Petro | Eoameloff | 1898 | Warland |
| Vasil | Esmirlieff | 1870 | Lombard |
| Numo | Etscoff | 1876 | Warland |
| Petro | Eunoff | 1880 | Warland |
| Tony | Evanoff | 1888 | N/A |
| Christ | Evanoff | 1899 | Missoula |
| Trayo | Evanoff | 1895 | Mineral |
| Lambro | Evanoff | 1881 | Miles City |
| Tom | Evanoff | 1896 | Cascade |
| Jim George | Evanoff | 1888 | Butte |
| Delin | Evanoff | 1893 | Bowdoin |
| Naum | Evanoff | 1867 | Rosebud |
| George D.H. | Evanoff | N/A | Butte |
| James | Evanoff | 1895 | Cold Springs |
| Svetco | Evanoff | 1881 | Great Falls |
| Demo | Evanoff | 1881 | Missoula |
| Milan | Evanoff | 1884 | N/A |
| Evan N. | Evanoff | 1874 | Hill |
| Christ | Evanoff | 1896 | Havre |
| Nicola | Evanoff | 1882 | Jefferson |
| Done | Evanoff | 1877 | N/A |
| Tony | Evanoff | 1875 | Butte |
| Tony | Evanoff | 1882 | Great Falls |
| Jasto | Evanoff | 1887 | Lombard |
| Nick | Evanoff | 1884 | Neihart |
| Gabriel | Evanoff | 1896 | Hill |
| Naum | Evanoff | 1893 | Blaine |
| Vasil | Evanoff | 1894 | Blaine |
| Nick | Evanoff | 1891 | N/A |
| Daniel | Evans | 1898 | Lewistown |
| Stavro | Evansoff | 1898 | Warland |
| Simion | Evenoff | 1882 | Fergus |
| Vasil | Evenoff | 1889 | Fergus |
| Nick | Evonoff | 1890 | Cottonwood |

| | | | |
|---|---|---|---|
| Ato | Fileheff | 1865 | Lombard |
| Pepaud | Filleff | 1891 | Armington |
| Elisa | Foleff | 1891 | Great Falls |
| John | Foleff | 1912 | Great Falls |
| C. | Galagachiff | 1875 | Box Elder |
| John | Gamell | 1888 | Lewistown |
| Louis | Gamell | 1914 | Lewistown |
| Sultana | Gamell (Liazeva) | N/A | Lewistown |
| Nick | Garloff | 1892 | Silver Bow |
| Frank | Gaunos | 1880 | Armington |
| Tony | Gechoff | 1873 | Miles City |
| Christ | Gennoff | 1883 | Saltese |
| Nick | George | 1875 | Meagher |
| Pete | George | 1895 | Billings |
| Nick | George | N/A | Dawson |
| Crist | George | 1892 | Meagher |
| Take | George | 1880 | Glasgow |
| Nick | George | 1889 | Lewistown |
| Christ | George | 1891 | Little Porcupine |
| Frank D. | George | 1871 | Melstone |
| Nurmi | George | N/A | Missoula |
| Fate | George | N/A | Dawson |
| Pete | George | 1885 | Fergus |
| Dicko | Georgeff | 1871 | Bowdoin |
| Kristo | Georgeoff | 1885 | Warland |
| Kirco | Georgergenoff | 1887 | Saltese |
| Demetry | Georgiaff | 1872 | Rosebud |
| Lazo | Gergoff | 1882 | Warland |
| Pete | Geroge | 1893 | Missoula |
| Nick | Geyton | 1862 | Fergus |
| Nicklas | Ginoff | 1894 | Lincoln |
| Peter | Ginoff | 1896 | N/A |
| Thomas | Ginoff | N/A | N/A |
| Steve | Gonga | 1892 | Williamsburg |
| Kasma | Gorge | N/A | Dawson |

| | | | |
|---|---|---|---|
| Jemey | Gorge | N/A | Dawson |
| Jasp | Gorge | N/A | Dawson |
| Mike | Gorge | N/A | Dawson |
| A. | Gouroukoff | 1860 | Box Elder |
| S. | Gouroukoff | 1870 | Box Elder |
| C. | Gouroukoff | 1888 | Box Elder |
| A. | Gouroukoff | 1890 | Box Elder |
| John | Grass | 1886 | Treasure |
| Spiro | Guloff | 1874 | Rosebud |
| Risto | Gusta | 1875 | Fergus |
| Loy | Gusta | 1886 | Fergus |
| George | Gwendeff | 1885 | Lombard |
| Christ | Hantonoff | 1887 | Saltese |
| James | Haranpalis | 1881 | Yellowstone |
| Christ | Hlebaroff | 1887 | Livingston |
| Steve | Holeff | 1889 | Butte |
| George | Hulera | N/A | Butte |
| Eliea | Inkoff | 1868 | Ferus |
| Lemon | Irikoff | 1883 | Meagher |
| Dimitri | Ivanoff | 1882 | Charlo |
| Dennis | James | 1895 | Three Forks |
| Van | Janott | 1898 | Butte |
| John | Jeorgeff | 1887 | Lombard |
| Sterio | Jepip | N/A | Dawson |
| Slaron | Jepo | N/A | Dawson |
| Leoneda | Jisoff | N/A | Dawson |
| Phillip | Joe | 1878 | Lewis and Clark |
| Meyik | John | 1878 | Armington |
| Steve | John | 1885 | Armington |
| Jim | John | 1888 | Fergus |
| Nick | John | 1894 | Custer |
| Steve | John | 1885 | Cottonwood |
| Frank | Johnoff | 1892 | Miles City |
| Thatel | Jorgeff | 1888 | Chinook |
| Metode | Joseaf | 1883 | Armington |

| | | | |
|---|---|---|---|
| Dimitri | Jreoff | 1887 | Lombard |
| Mik | Jriagr | 1886 | Lombard |
| Thri | Jrorgr | 1865 | Lombard |
| Nick | Jrorgr | 1868 | Lombard |
| Gust | Juloff | 1891 | Evaro |
| Criso | Kairro | 1884 | Superior |
| Daman | Kakoff | 1898 | Chouteau |
| Apostol E. | Kakoff | 1888 | Denton |
| Tanka | Kakoff | N/A | Denton |
| Louis | Kakoff | N/A | Denton |
| Vasil | Kalchoff | 1873 | Warland |
| Numo | Kalcoff | 1880 | Warland |
| Nasi | Kalfstoff | 1887 | Lombard |
| Ulora | Kalmuoff | 1873 | Deer Lodge |
| Dini | Kalstoff | 1887 | Lombard |
| Apostle | Kamioski | 1885 | Charlo |
| Dium | Karadgoff | 1891 | Lombard |
| Laso | Karaeff | 1885 | Lombard |
| Dimche | Karamsoff | 1888 | Lombard |
| Dini | Karinkich | 1885 | Lombard |
| Vasil | Kaschoff | 1885 | Warland |
| Louis | Kastoff | 1891 | Dawson |
| Nick | Kaugaff | 1898 | Malmberg |
| Lotko | Keeroff | 1899 | Charlo |
| Elia | Kilmanoff | 1873 | Charlo |
| Pete | Kirazoff | 1896 | Deer Lodge |
| Pasko | Kirizoff | 1897 | Charlo |
| Christo | Kiroff | 1878 | Rosebud |
| Nazo | Kirro | 1898 | Superior |
| George | Kisoff | 1872 | Box Elder |
| Pando | Kita | 1874 | Deer Lodge |
| Christ | Kiutenoff | 1887 | Armington |
| Vido | Kiymonoff | 1890 | Harlowton |
| Pete | Klimoff | 1884 | Armington |
| Pasko | Klimoff | 1888 | Armington |

| | | | |
|---|---|---|---|
| Angelo | Kochoff | 1880 | Meagher |
| Nikola | Koleshoff | 1880 | Fergus |
| Diui | Kolioff | 1885 | Lombard |
| Ilia | Koloff | 1880 | Lombard |
| Apostol | Komiorsky | 1884 | Deer Lodge |
| Usco | Kossap | 1890 | Meagher |
| Louis | Kostoff | 1891 | Dawson |
| John | Kostoff | N/A | Butte |
| Louis | Kostoff | 1890 | Deer Lodge |
| Teofil | Kostoff | 1894 | Mineral |
| Mike | Kostos | 1888 | Butte |
| John | Kosty | 1885 | Miles City |
| Mary | Kosty | 1886 | Miles City |
| Christopher | Kosty | 1908 | Miles City |
| Andre | Kozma | 1887 | Armington |
| Evan | Kramsoff | 1889 | Lombard |
| Peter H. | Kreste | 1883 | Hamilton |
| Mamis | Kristoff | N/A | Dawson |
| Pete | Kriszto | 1877 | North |
| Zlatko | Kroll | 1898 | Deer Lodge |
| Pete | Kurtiff | 1865 | Butte |
| Stoko | Kuszoff | 1887 | Park |
| Evan | Lambroff | 1879 | Rosebud |
| Harri | Lappas | 1896 | Charlo |
| Mike N. | Lappas | 1885 | Charlo |
| George | Lardroff | 1887 | Rosebud |
| George D. | Lashoff | 1872 | Savoy |
| John | Lazar | 1860 | Miles City |
| Panaist | Lazaroff | 1887 | Poplar |
| Andon | Lazaroff | 1875 | Rosebud |
| Christ | Lazaroff | 1873 | Rosebud |
| Naum | Lazaroff | 1880 | Bowdoin |
| Stavro | Lazaroff | 1900 | Ferus |
| Antone | Lazaroff | 1885 | Warland |
| Gele | Lazoff | 1872 | Butte |

| | | | |
|---|---|---|---|
| Nick | Lazoff | 1895 | N/A |
| George | Lebiy | 1870 | Lewis and Clark |
| Stero | Leshoff | N/A | Dawson |
| Alexander | Lodinoff | 1888 | Whitefish |
| George | Louis | N/A | Dawson |
| Dini | Lousheff | 1887 | Lombard |
| Louis | Luchis | 1893 | Butte |
| George | Makedonski | N/A | N/A |
| Jamp | Maku | N/A | Dawson |
| Spiro | Malisory | 1893 | St. Regis |
| Theodore | Mano | N/A | Butte |
| Jim | Masteff | 1870 | Lombard |
| Geovan | Mattoff | N/A | Dawson |
| Stario | Mekaf | N/A | Dawson |
| Stoyan | Meloff | 1872 | Butte |
| Dushon | Meshee | 1892 | Meagher |
| Christ | Methell | 1897 | Miles City |
| Gliroffalie | Metreff | 1887 | Armington |
| Christ | Metroff | 1885 | Choteau |
| Steve | Metroff | 1886 | Warland |
| Lapo | Metseff | N/A | Dawson |
| Nasi | Migleneff | 1892 | Lombard |
| Nupufof | Mikail | N/A | Dawson |
| George | Mike | 1880 | Cottonwood |
| Paul | Mike | 1888 | Hobson |
| Jime | Mike | 1870 | Charlo |
| Katherine | Mike | 1910 | Hobson |
| Donna | Mike (Eftoff) | N/A | Hobson |
| Ziss | Mikoloff | 1898 | Deer Lodge |
| Eli | Mileff | 1888 | Prarie |
| Eli | Miliff | 1892 | Corbin |
| Tonny | Miloff | 1885 | Miles City |
| Theodore | Mistoff | 1896 | Whitefish |
| Geroge | Mitreff | 1889 | Saltese |
| Blagoye | Mitsareff | 1890 | N/A |

| | | | |
|---|---|---|---|
| Christopher | Mitsif | 1887 | Chinook |
| Lester | Moschas | 1892 | Charlo |
| Lester | Mosches | 1892 | Deer Lodge |
| Cristo | Nago | 1876 | Meagher |
| Bill | Nakoff | 1894 | Rosebud |
| Atanas | Nakoff | 1885 | Rosebud |
| Lazar | Nanoff | 1887 | Frazer |
| Nice | Nanoff | 1893 | Yellowstone |
| Christ | Naso | 1897 | Corbin |
| Allia | Naumaff | N/A | Dawson |
| Naso | Naumoff | 1892 | Cobury |
| George | Naumoff | 1871 | Rosebud |
| Temeles | Naumoff | 1878 | Butte |
| Lazo | Naumoff | 1876 | Butte |
| Nass | Naumoff | 1897 | Butte |
| Atans | Naumoff | 1893 | Ingomar |
| George | Naurny | 1886 | Corbin |
| Eli | Nesteroff | 1872 | Warland |
| Anthony | Nicholas | 1883 | Chinook |
| Kosto | Nicholoff | N/A | Roundup |
| Gus | Nichols | 1893 | Superior |
| Mike | Nick | N/A | Dawson |
| Christ | Nick | 1888 | Fergus |
| George | Nickoloff | 1893 | Brockton |
| Diana | Nickoloff | 1907 | Brockton |
| Kosta | Nickoloff | 1883 | Mondak |
| Tasco | Nicolesco | 1874 | Lewistown |
| George | Nicoloff | 1889 | Meagher |
| Stoan | Nicoloff | 1884 | Deer Lodge |
| Nassa | Nicoloff | 1884 | Charlo |
| Izesu | Nicoloff | 1902 | Charlo |
| George | Nicoloff | 1873 | Great Falls |
| Vargell | Nikaloff | 1885 | Deer Lodge |
| Alex | Nikoloff | 1892 | Fergus |
| Vani | Nikoloff | 1888 | Lombard |

| | | | |
|---|---|---|---|
| Ela | Niladenoff | 1873 | Yellowstone |
| Christ | Ninkola | 1875 | Lombard |
| Kiril | Noleff | 1897 | Butte |
| Anthony | Nonnoff | 1889 | Saltese |
| George | Noram | 1885 | Armington |
| Elia | Noumoff | 1887 | Poplar |
| Christ | Numoff | 1868 | Wolf Point |
| Nikola | Orgiroff | 1892 | Lombard |
| Gogo | Otseff | 1871 | Meagher |
| Peter N. | Palasco | 1891 | Whitefish |
| Danl | Pandoff | 1878 | Rosebud |
| George | Pandoff | 1895 | Great Falls |
| George | Pandolf | 1897 | Missoula |
| Micko | Papasev | N/A | Dawson |
| Lambo | Papoff | 1888 | Bearmouth |
| Peter | Pappas | 1896 | Billings |
| Costa | Pariza | 1889 | Butte |
| Anthony | Parrish | 1894 | Hamilton |
| Tom | Paskoff | 1887 | Lombard |
| Nisi | Paskoff | 1892 | Lombard |
| Tom | Paul | 1888 | Deer Lodge |
| Steven P. | Paul | 1883 | Warland |
| Angel | Pavliff | 1882 | Cottonwood |
| Anton | Pavloff | 1867 | Rosebud |
| Vasil | Pentsoff | 1894 | Warland |
| Aristo | Pereloff | 1882 | Warland |
| Same | Peroski | 1887 | Charlo |
| John | Pete | 1888 | Armington |
| Jim | Pete | 1894 | Butte |
| Chris O. | Petkoff | 1885 | Lombard |
| Stoley | Petro | 1887 | Meagher |
| Sam | Petroff | 1891 | Glasgow |
| Caloto | Petroff | 1868 | Bearmouth |
| Ev. P. | Petroff | 1890 | Lombard |
| Mike | Petsoff | 1882 | Cottonwood |

| | | | |
|---|---|---|---|
| Lambro | Philip | 1898 | Wolf Point |
| Vane | Phillips | 1886 | Lewistown |
| Louis | Phillips | 1889 | Valier |
| Anton | Pirovsky | 1873 | Rosebud |
| Christ | Pirovsky | 1882 | Rosebud |
| Sam | Poiskoff | 1887 | Deer Lodge |
| Levi Mike | Poluso | 1876 | Butte |
| Pasku | Popeka | 1888 | Plentywood |
| Jim | Popeka | N/A | Plentywood |
| Tache Jim | Popescu | N/A | Plentywood |
| George | Popoff | 1897 | Rosebud |
| Kuzo | Popoff | 1864 | Wolf Point |
| Kocho | Popoff | 1870 | Lombard |
| Nick | Popoff | 1888 | Lombard |
| Vasil | Popoff | 1872 | Warland |
| George | Popoff | 1875 | Warland |
| Blago | Popoff | 1900 | Warland |
| Vois | Poporsky | 1892 | Lombard |
| Mito | Poporsky | 1892 | Lombard |
| Lajo | Popovsku | 1875 | Lombard |
| Phrist | Pruvf | 1887 | Yellowstone |
| Deno | Raramanoff | 1891 | Lombard |
| George | Regins | 1891 | Ravalli |
| Vasil | Reskovsky | 1873 | Rosebud |
| John | Ristoff | 1882 | Miles City |
| Naumka | Ristoff | 1881 | Miles City |
| Louie | Ristoff | N/A | Miles City |
| Satic | Robeff | 1885 | Bearmouth |
| Louis | Rufoff | 1897 | Rosebud |
| L | Samanoff | 1882 | Box Elder |
| A | Samanoff | 1885 | Box Elder |
| Chris | Saroff | 1875 | Miles City |
| Lamera | Sateroff | 1871 | Rosebud |
| Nick | Satir | 1870 | Lombard |
| Vasel | Savacas | N/A | Dawson |

| | | | |
|---|---|---|---|
| Joe | Schicley | 1882 | Helena |
| Apastle | Schmmanoff | 1887 | Warm Springs |
| Nick | Serbinoff | 1890 | Missoula |
| Micho | Shamahoff | 1883 | Poplar |
| William K. | Shamanoff | 1901 | Great Falls |
| Apostalis | Shangaris | 1891 | Bitter Root Valley |
| Chris | Shishkoff | 1875 | Lombard |
| Saler | Shomaff | N/A | Dawson |
| Norman | Shotnokoff | 1893 | N/A |
| Sotir | Sichanoff | 1885 | Miles City |
| Thomy | Sichanoff | 1900 | Miles City |
| Nikolif | Simonoff | 1888 | N/A |
| Nick | Sincheff | 1871 | Rosebud |
| Boris | Sincheff | 1900 | Rosebud |
| Steve | Skokloff | 1898 | Bowdoin |
| Chris | Sotir | 1892 | Butte |
| Svetar | Sotscoff | 1873 | Miles City |
| Aresto | Sperro | 1866 | Meagher |
| Stosa | Spiroff | 1882 | Belmont |
| Christ D. | Spiroff | 1881 | Belmont |
| Nick | Spiroff | 1891 | Fergus |
| Nicola | Spiroff | 1890 | Valentine |
| Eli | Spuroff | 1889 | Meagher |
| Steve | Stamoff | 1895 | Chouteau |
| Poncho | Stanicheff | 1874 | Warland |
| Petro | Stankoff | 1893 | Rosebud |
| Paul | Stankoff | 1875 | Yellowstone |
| George | Stanoff | 1895 | Cascade |
| Louie | Stanoff | 1896 | Butte |
| Arger | Starraff | N/A | Dawson |
| Mito | Stavroff | 1887 | Lombard |
| Stase | Stazonoff | 1877 | Wolf Point |
| Ev. P. | Sterioff | 1887 | Lombard |
| Jip | Steris | N/A | Dawson |
| Louis | Steyanoff | 1897 | Charlo |

| Elia | Stoionoff | 1896 | Deer Lodge |
|---|---|---|---|
| Christ | Stonoff | 1859 | Corbin |
| Kacho | Stoycheff | 1870 | Lombard |
| Evan | Stoytchoff | 1862 | Fergus |
| Vanie | Taheff | 1880 | Fergus |
| Naum K. | Taleff | N/A | Superior |
| Todor | Taleff | 1882 | Missoula |
| Aspesia | Taleff (Alexandrova) | N/A | Superior |
| Trpe | Tanas | 1871 | Bearmouth |
| Philip | Tanas | 1893 | Great Falls |
| Hase | Tanascoff | 1887 | Butte |
| Christo | Tanaskoff | 1887 | Fergus |
| S.D. | Tanaskoff | 1886 | Fergus |
| John | Taneas | 1878 | Armington |
| Dunstri | Taptchiff | 1886 | Cottonwood |
| Mitro | Tarpanian | 1882 | Warland |
| Nome | Tarpo | 1886 | Butte |
| Chris | Tarpo | 1890 | Harlowton |
| Dina | Tarpo | 1890 | Harlowton |
| Vangel | Tarpof | N/A | Dawson |
| Ilia | Tasaff | 1877 | Saltese |
| Lepo | Taseff | 1875 | Rosebud |
| Otso | Taseff | 1877 | Saltese |
| George | Taseff | 1875 | Rosebud |
| Etso | Taseff | 1896 | Hill |
| Geroge | Tashev | N/A | Dawson |
| Louis | Tashoff | 1891 | Custer |
| Phillip | Tauar | 1897 | Corbin |
| Nicoli | Tepoff | 1862 | Fergus |
| Paul M. | Terzioff | 1896 | Deer Lodge |
| Kiril | Terzioff | 1894 | Deer Lodge |
| Marion | Thapin | 1889 | Little Porcupine |
| Alexandre | Thodoroff | 1884 | Cottonwood |
| Gus | Thomas | 1893 | Corbin |

| | | | |
|---|---|---|---|
| Nick | Thompson | 1887 | Great Falls |
| Soter | Timoff | 1873 | Bowdoin |
| Dimul | Toko | 1886 | Chinook |
| Nick K. | Toleff | 1882 | Havre |
| Louis | Toleff | 1894 | Great Falls |
| Elo | Toleff | 1892 | Chouteau |
| Vone | Toleff | 1879 | Fergus |
| Mitro | Tomiff | 1898 | Warland |
| Cris | Tony | 1893 | Fergus |
| Fene | Torett | 1890 | Fergus |
| Jim | Torofiffoff | 1897 | Geraldine |
| Tony | Tossiff | 1869 | Meagher |
| Chi | Toucoff | 1887 | Lombard |
| Dini | Trapehanoff | 1887 | Lombard |
| Dinco | Traukoff | 1880 | Corbin |
| James | Tricoff | 1894 | Butte |
| John | Tricolt | 1890 | Butte |
| Tom | Triff | 1881 | Lewistown |
| Elisa | Turff | 1873 | Treasure |
| Dini | Uanoff | 1875 | Lombard |
| Mike | Ulani | 1884 | Butte |
| Atanes | Vane | 1884 | Fergus |
| Nass | Vangelof | N/A | Dawson |
| Nick | Vangelof | N/A | Dawson |
| James | Vanoff | 1882 | Malmberg |
| Thomas | Varne | 1890 | Big Porcupine |
| Limlo | Varne | 1880 | Big Porcupine |
| George | Vasampalis | 1885 | Yellowstone |
| Ary | Vasels | N/A | Dawson |
| Tarhe | Vasikell | 1880 | Deer Lodge |
| Pando | Vasilaff | 1889 | Blaine |
| Jim | Vasileff | 1895 | Silver Bow |
| Nikola | Vasileff | 1882 | Bearmouth |
| Jim | Vasileff | 1887 | Lombard |
| Naum | Vasileff | 1891 | Lombard |

| | | | |
|---|---|---|---|
| James | Vasileff | 1899 | Malmberg |
| George | Vasiliov | 1890 | Butte |
| James | Vasiliow | 1892 | Black Eagle |
| Dimiter | Vasill | 1885 | Rosebud |
| John | Vasille | 1893 | Granite |
| Theodoro | Vasiloff | 1886 | Deer Lodge |
| Theodore | Vasiloff | 1887 | Charlo |
| Turpo | Vasiloff | 1880 | Charlo |
| Spero | Vasiloff | 1899 | Warland |
| John | Vassie | 1880 | Meagher |
| Harry | Vassil | 1891 | Cascade |
| Gus | Veloff | 1879 | Lewis and Clark |
| Christ | Verchoff | 1871 | Miles City |
| James | Vinlerr | 1897 | Williamsburg |
| Lotur | Wandriee | 1872 | Meagher |
| Thushi | Wangel | 1880 | Armington |
| Maik | Wlom | N/A | Dawson |
| Mary | Yankoff | 1882 | Miles City |
| Pano | Yosivoff | 1890 | Melstone |
| Dimitre | Yranoff | 1883 | Deer Lodge |
| Lazarus | Zandanoff | 1886 | Charlo |
| Lazar | Zardenoff | 1885 | Deer Lodge |
| Christ | Zekoff | 1884 | Deer Lodge |
| Steve | Zerincheff | 1882 | Cottonwood |
| Blago | Zesoff | 1892 | Warland |
| Christ | Ziekoff | 1895 | Charlo |
| Steve | Zirineheff | 1867 | Elk Park |
| Angele | Zlatiff | 1884 | Cottonwood |
| Anton C. | Zugloff | 1878 | Missoula |
| Stasho | Zugloff | 1894 | Missoula |
| Elia | Zugloff | 1895 | Missoula |

# ENDNOTES

[1] This nickname for Montana was popularized by the Montana State Highway Department in the 1960s and originated in a novel titled Big Sky, written by Alfred B. Guthrie Jr. in 1947. https://statesymbolsusa.org/symbol-official-item/montana/state-nickname/treasure-state

[2] Christowe, Stoyan, *This is My Country*, (Carrick & Evans: New York, 1938), Pg. 85.

[3] Christowe, Stoyan, *This is My Country*, (Carrick & Evans: New York, 1938), Pg. 85.

[4] Albert Sonnichsen claimed in 1909 that 10,000 "Bulgars from Bulgaria and Macedonia" were, in 1909, working on the railroads "in Montana, the two Dakotas, Iowa and Minnesota." He said about 8,000 of these men originated from Macedonia. See Balch, Emily G., *Our Slavic Fellow Citizens*, (Charities Publication Committee: New York, 1910), Pg. 274, 275.

[5] It must be noted that, in this context, 'Macedonian' refers to any individual who was born in geographical Macedonia, which today is located primarily in three countries: Republic of Macedonia (Vardar Macedonia), southwestern Bulgaria (Pirin Macedonia), and northern Greece (Aegean Macedonia). It does not refer to American-born individuals with Macedonian ancestry.

[6] "United States World War I Draft Registration Cards, 1917-1918," database with images, FamilySearch (https://familysearch.org/ark:/61903/1:1:K689-FTY : 13 March 2018), Lazar Kostoff Nanoff, 1917-1918; citing Corson County, South Dakota, United States, NARA microfilm publication M1509 (Washington D.C.: National Archives and Records Administration, n.d.); FHL microfilm 1,877,789.

[7] "United States World War I Draft Registration Cards, 1917-1918," database with images, FamilySearch (https://familysearch.org/ark:/61903/1:1:K8QJ-M2Z : 13 March 2018), Alexander Dimitroff, 1917-1918; citing Missoula County, Montana, United States, NARA microfilm publication M1509 (Washington D.C.: National Archives and Records Administration, n.d.); FHL microfilm 1,711,436.

[8] "United States World War I Draft Registration Cards, 1917-1918," database with images, FamilySearch (https://familysearch.org/ark:/61903/1:1:K8QJ-6QG : 13 March 2018), Christ Hlebaroff, 1917-1918; citing Park County, Montana, United States, NARA microfilm publication M1509 (Washington D.C.: National Archives and Records Administration, n.d.); FHL microfilm 1,711,438.

[9] https://www.findagrave.com/memorial/60976273

[10] "United States World War I Draft Registration Cards, 1917-1918," database with images, FamilySearch (https://familysearch.org/ark:/61903/1:1:K8QN-6FV : 13 March 2018), Vane Christoff, 1917-1918; citing Fergus County, Montana, United States, NARA microfilm publication M1509 (Washington D.C.: National Archives and Records Administration, n.d.); FHL microfilm 1,684,112.

[11] "United States Census, 1920," database with images, FamilySearch (https://familysearch.org/ark:/61903/1:1:M832-66W : accessed 28 December 2018), Thomas Triff, School District 1, Fergus, Montana, United States; citing ED 84, sheet 13B, line 82, family 277, NARA microfilm publication T625 (Washington D.C.: National Archives and Records Administration, 1992), roll 969; FHL microfilm 1,820,969.

[12] "United States World War I Draft Registration Cards, 1917-1918," database with images, FamilySearch (https://familysearch.org/ark:/61903/1:1:K8QJ-Z1L : 13 March 2018), Tom Triff, 1917-1918; citing Musselshell County, Montana, United States, NARA microfilm publication M1509 (Washington D.C.: National Archives and Records Administration, n.d.); FHL microfilm 1,711,437.

[13] "A Man Without a Country," The Daily Missoulian (Missoula, Montana) 06 Jun 1917, Page 5

[14] Sinadinoski, Dusan, "Macedonian Yankees in WWI," May 25, 2010; "Enemy Aliens and Interment," https://encyclopedia.1914-1918-online.net/article/enemy_aliens_and_internment

[15] Balch, Emily G., *Our Slavic Fellow Citizens*, (Charities Publication Committee: New York, 1910), Pg. 274, 275.

[16] Balch, Emily G., *Our Slavic Fellow Citizens*, (Charities Publication Committee: New York, 1910), Pg. 275, 276.

[17] *Instructions to Enumerators*, Thirteenth Census of the United States, April 15, 1910, (Government Printing Office: Washington, 1910), Pg. 32.

[18] *Instructions to Enumerators*, Fourteenth Census of the United States, (Government Printing Office: Washington, 1919), Pg. 31; *Instructions to Enumerators*, Fifteenth Census of the United States, (Government Printing Office: Washington, 1930), Pg. 30.

[19] *Instructions to Enumerators*, Sixteenth Decennial Census of the United States, (U.S. Department of Congress: Washington, 1940), Pg. 75. 76.

[20] *Instructions to Enumerators*, Fifteenth Census of the United States, (Government Printing Office: Washington, 1930), Pg. 30.

[21] "Men Kiss Each Other," Alton Evening Telegraph (Alton, Illinois), Oct 30, 1912, Page 7

[22] Trouton, Ruth, *Peasant Renaissance in Yugoslav, 1900-1950: A Study of the Development of Yugoslav Peasant Society as Affected by Education*, (London: Routledge, 1952, 1998), Pg. 96.

[23] "United States Census, 1920," database with images, FamilySearch (https://familysearch.org/ark:/61903/1:1:M8QH-P3Y : accessed 27 December 2018), Nick G Thompson, School District 21, Teton, Montana, United States; citing ED 211, sheet 6A, line 24, family 9, NARA microfilm publication T625 (Washington D.C.: National Archives and Records Administration, 1992), roll 977; FHL microfilm 1,820,977.

[24] "United States Census, 1940," database with images, FamilySearch (https://familysearch.org/ark:/61903/1:1:VB31-N78 : 16 March 2018), James

Christoff, Belton Township, Flathead, Montana, United States; citing enumeration district (ED) 15-1, sheet 3A, line 17, family 63, Sixteenth Census of the United States, 1940, NARA digital publication T627. Records of the Bureau of the Census, 1790 - 2007, RG 29. Washington, D.C.: National Archives and Records Administration, 2012, roll 2219; "United States World War I Draft Registration Cards, 1917-1918," database with images, FamilySearch (https://familysearch.org/ark:/61903/1:1:K8QJ-NX3 : 13 March 2018), James Christoff, 1917-1918; citing Phillips County, Montana, United States, NARA microfilm publication M1509 (Washington D.C.: National Archives and Records Administration, n.d.); FHL microfilm 1,711,438.

[25] "United States Census, 1940," database with images, FamilySearch (https://familysearch.org/ark:/61903/1:1:VBQF-HK8 : 13 March 2018), Lee Angeloff, School District 24 Hedgesville, Wheatland, Montana, United States; citing enumeration district (ED) 54-9, sheet 1A, line 36, family 11, Sixteenth Census of the United States, 1940, NARA digital publication T627. Records of the Bureau of the Census, 1790 - 2007, RG 29. Washington, D.C.: National Archives and Records Administration, 2012, roll 2233.

[26] "United States Census, 1940," database with images, FamilySearch (https://familysearch.org/ark:/61903/1:1:VBQQ-FL1 : 15 March 2018), James Tricoff, School District 18 Fulton, Lewis and Clark, Montana, United States; citing enumeration district (ED) 25-32, sheet 1A, line 23, family 7, Sixteenth Census of the United States, 1940, NARA digital publication T627. Records of the Bureau of the Census, 1790 - 2007, RG 29. Washington, D.C.: National Archives and Records Administration, 2012, roll 2222; "John Tricoff, 81, Dies in Dillon," The Montana Standard (Butte, Montana) 24 Oct 1975, Page 2

[27] "United States Census, 1940," database with images, FamilySearch (https://familysearch.org/ark:/61903/1:1:VBQM-N66 : 16 March 2018), Christ D Botaff, Whitefish, Whitefish Township, Flathead, Montana, United States; citing enumeration district (ED) 15-31, sheet 6A, line 27, family 163, Sixteenth Census of the United States, 1940, NARA digital publication T627. Records of the Bureau of the Census, 1790 - 2007, RG 29. Washington, D.C.: National Archives and Records Administration, 2012, roll 2219; "Find A Grave Index," database, FamilySearch (https://familysearch.org/ark:/61903/1:1:QVLC-TH9N : 13 December 2015), Christ Demetry Botaff, 1962; Burial, Whitefish, Flathead, Montana, United States of America, Whitefish Cemetery; citing record ID 91751242, Find a Grave, http://www.findagrave.com; "United States World War I Draft Registration Cards, 1917-1918," database with images, FamilySearch (https://familysearch.org/ark:/61903/1:1:K8QN-DNQ : 13 March 2018), Christ Demetry Botaff, 1917-1918; citing Fergus County, Montana, United States, NARA microfilm publication M1509 (Washington D.C.: National Archives and Records Administration, n.d.); FHL microfilm 1,684,112; "Christ Botaff Dies in Whitefish," The Missoulian (Missoula, Montana) 26 Jan 1962, Page 8

[28] "United States Census, 1940," database with images, FamilySearch (https://familysearch.org/ark:/61903/1:1:VB3Y-XQF : 15 March 2018), Tony Gechoff, School District 1 Miles City, Custer, Montana, United States; citing enumeration district (ED) 9-8, sheet 2B, line 48, family 35, Sixteenth Census of the United States, 1940, NARA digital publication T627. Records of the Bureau of the Census, 1790 - 2007, RG 29. Washington, D.C.: National Archives and Records Administration, 2012, roll 2216.

[29] "United States Census, 1930," database with images, FamilySearch (https://familysearch.org/ark:/61903/1:1:XC99-5PM : accessed 30 December 2018), Nass Naumoff in household of Diminik Nicolaoa, Butte, Silver Bow, Montana, United States; citing enumeration district (ED) ED 32, sheet 5A, line 48, family 72, NARA microfilm publication T626 (Washington D.C.: National Archives and Records Administration, 2002), roll 1262; FHL microfilm 2,340,997.

[30] Metody Batchoff, also of Butte from 1912 until 1932, when he died. "Batchoff Death," The Montana Standard (Butte, Montana) 14 Jun 1932, Page 5; "Montana, County Births and Deaths, 1840-2004," database with images, FamilySearch (https://familysearch.org/ark:/61903/1:1:QKNR-CRC9 : 4 August 2017), Metody A Batchoff, 13 Jun 1932; citing Death, Butte, Silver Bow, Montana, United States, various county recorder offices; FHL microfilm 2,311,842.

[31] Theodore Mano," The Montana Standard (Butte, Montana) 23 Sep 1949, Page 5

[32] "United States Census, 1940," database with images, FamilySearch (https://familysearch.org/ark:/61903/1:1:VBQW-YT7 : 15 March 2018), Pete George in household of Carl F Schwaeble, Election Precinct 37 Cold Springs, Missoula, Montana, United States; citing enumeration district (ED) 32-38, sheet 6A, line 8, family 117, Sixteenth Census of the United States, 1940, NARA digital publication T627. Records of the Bureau of the Census, 1790 - 2007, RG 29. Washington, D.C.: National Archives and Records Administration, 2012, roll 2225.

[33] Christowe, Stoyan, *The Eagle and the Stork*, (New York: Harpers Magazine Press, 1976), Pg. 67.

[34] "United States Census, 1920," database with images, FamilySearch (https://familysearch.org/ark:/61903/1:1:M83N-DVM : accessed 28 December 2018), Angelo Angilofsky, Great Falls Ward 1, Cascade, Montana, United States; citing ED 14, sheet 9B, line 69, family 208, NARA microfilm publication T625 (Washington D.C.: National Archives and Records Administration, 1992), roll 968; FHL microfilm 1,820,968.

[35] "Truman Names Batchoff as Marshal," The Independent-Record (Helena, Montana) 08 Mar 1949, Page 1

[36] "Montana, Military Records, 1904-1918," database, FamilySearch (https://familysearch.org/ark:/61903/1:1:QPL2-4PWM : 2 November 2018), Nicola Andanoff, 30 Apr 1918; citing Military Service, Duluth, St. Louis, Minnesota, United States, Montana State Historical Society, Helena.

[37] "Montana, Military Records, 1904-1918," database, FamilySearch (https://familysearch.org/ark:/61903/1:1:QP2Z-GDTJ : 2 November 2018), Nikolif Simonoff, 14 Dec 1917; citing Military Service, Mineral, Montana, United States, Montana State Historical Society, Helena.

[38] "Montana, Military Records, 1904-1918," database, FamilySearch (https://familysearch.org/ark:/61903/1:1:QPKR-GB9J : 2 November 2018), Blagoye D Mitsareff, 25 Jun 1918; citing Military Service, Valley, Montana, United States, Montana State Historical Society, Helena.

[39] "Montana, Military Records, 1904-1918," database, FamilySearch (https://familysearch.org/ark:/61903/1:1:QPRC-2W1N : 2 November 2018), Nick Serbinoff, 30 Aug 1917; citing Military Service, Missoula, Montana, United States, Montana State Historical Society, Helena.

[40] "Montana, Military Records, 1904-1918," database, FamilySearch (https://familysearch.org/ark:/61903/1:1:QPLR-V7WR : 2 November 2018), Costa G. Pariza, 2 Jul 1918; citing Military Service, Montgomery, Virginia, United States, Montana State Historical Society, Helena.

[41] "Costa Pariza, 97," The Montana Standard (Butte, Montana) 05 Jan 1987, Page 2

[42] "Montana, Military Records, 1904-1918," database, FamilySearch (https://familysearch.org/ark:/61903/1:1:QP2Z-T4QH : 2 November 2018), Christ Sotir, 27 May 1918; citing Military Service, Butte, Silver Bow, Montana, United States, Montana State Historical Society, Helena.

[43] "Montana, Military Records, 1904-1918," database, FamilySearch (https://familysearch.org/ark:/61903/1:1:QP2C-3S1N : 2 November 2018), Christ Eftinoff, 30 Jun 1918; citing Military Service, Miles City, Custer, Montana, United States, Montana State Historical Society, Helena.

[44] "Montana, Military Records, 1904-1918," database, FamilySearch (https://familysearch.org/ark:/61903/1:1:QPLK-J25N : 2 November 2018), Philip Tanas, 26 Jul 1918; citing Military Service, Great Falls, Cascade, Montana, United States, Montana State Historical Society, Helena.

[45] "Montana, Military Records, 1904-1918," database, FamilySearch (https://familysearch.org/ark:/61903/1:1:QP2Z-8HNH : 2 November 2018), Spiro T Malisory, 18 Sep 1917; citing Military Service, Superior, Mineral, Montana, United States, Montana State Historical Society, Helena.

[46] "Montana, Military Records, 1904-1918," database, FamilySearch (https://familysearch.org/ark:/61903/1:1:QP5G-7S6T : 2 November 2018), Pano T Yosivoff, 26 Aug 1918; citing Military Service, Musselshell, Montana, United States, Montana State Historical Society, Helena.

[47] "Montana, Military Records, 1904-1918," database, FamilySearch (https://familysearch.org/ark:/61903/1:1:QPL5-RC2Y : 2 November 2018), Nick George, 20 Sep 1917; citing Military Service, Lewistown, Fergus, Montana, United States, Montana State Historical Society, Helena.

[48] "Montana, Military Records, 1904-1918," database, FamilySearch (https://familysearch.org/ark:/61903/1:1:QPPX-1K79 : 2 November 2018), Ted G Christ, 29 May 1918; citing Military Service, Cascade, Montana, United States, Montana State Historical Society, Helena.

[49] "Montana, Military Records, 1904-1918," database, FamilySearch (https://familysearch.org/ark:/61903/1:1:QPLV-9TD6 : 2 November 2018), Peter Pappas, 29 Apr 1918; citing Military Service, Montana, United States, Montana State Historical Society, Helena.

[50] "Montana, Military Records, 1904-1918," database, FamilySearch (https://familysearch.org/ark:/61903/1:1:QP24-R61G : 2 November 2018), Vasil Aleexoff, 11 Feb 1918; citing Military Service, St. Louis, Missouri, United States, Montana State Historical Society, Helena.

[51] "Montana, Military Records, 1904-1918," database, FamilySearch (https://familysearch.org/ark:/61903/1:1:QP5B-Z242 : 2 November 2018), Stasho G Zugloff, 3 Nov 1917; citing Military Service, Missoula, Montana, United States, Montana State Historical Society, Helena.

[52] "Montana, Military Records, 1904-1918," database, FamilySearch (https://familysearch.org/ark:/61903/1:1:QPL2-D966 : 2 November 2018), Tom Basil, 7 Oct 1917; citing Military Service, Philipsburg, Granite, Montana, United States, Montana State Historical Society, Helena.

[53] "Montana, Military Records, 1904-1918," database, FamilySearch (https://familysearch.org/ark:/61903/1:1:QPPF-SXTB : 2 November 2018), Svetco Evanoff, 1 Sep 1917; citing Military Service, Klickitat, Klickitat, Washington, United States, Montana State Historical Society, Helena.

[54] "Montana, Military Records, 1904-1918," database, FamilySearch (https://familysearch.org/ark:/61903/1:1:QPPC-7MX8 : 2 November 2018), Gust Chreest, 31 May 1918; citing Military Service, St. Louis, Missouri, United States, Montana State Historical Society, Helena.

[55] "Nurmi George," The Missoulian (Missoula, Montana) 05 Jan 1941, Page 4

[56] "Rigged Wedding Goes 50 Years," The Montana Standard (Butte, Montana) 19 Sep 1971, Page 20

[57] Metody A. Batchoff," The Montana Standard (Butte, Montana) 16 Jun 1932, Page 8

[58] "N.G. Thompson, 55, Dies Here," Great Falls Tribune (Great Falls, Montana) 07 Nov 1946, Page 6

[59] "Gamell Rites Saturday," Great Falls Tribune (Great Falls, Montana) 29 Jan 1943, Page 12

[60] https://www.findagrave.com/memorial/81056128/matrona-angeloff#view-photo=85666012

[61] "United States Census, 1940," database with images, FamilySearch (https://familysearch.org/ark:/61903/1:1:VBQF-HK8 : 13 March 2018), Lee Angeloff, School District 24 Hedgesville, Wheatland, Montana, United States; citing enumeration district (ED) 54-9, sheet 1A, line 36, family 11, Sixteenth

Census of the United States, 1940, NARA digital publication T627. Records of the Bureau of the Census, 1790 - 2007, RG 29. Washington, D.C.: National Archives and Records Administration, 2012, roll 2233; "United States Census, 1920," database with images, FamilySearch (https://familysearch.org/ark:/61903/1:1:M83B-Q2Q : accessed 27 December 2018), Lee G Angeloff, School District 20, Musselshell, Montana, United States; citing ED 76, sheet 2B, line 63, family 46, NARA microfilm publication T625 (Washington D.C.: National Archives and Records Administration, 1992), roll 973; FHL microfilm 1,820,973;"Find A Grave Index," database, FamilySearch (https://familysearch.org/ark:/61903/1:1:QV2F-NWYT : 13 December 2015), Lee George Angeloff, 1956; Burial, , Wheatland, Montana, United States of America, Harlowton Cemetery; citing record ID 68694240, Find a Grave, http://www.findagrave.com; "Montana Death Index, 1860-2007," database, FamilySearch (https://familysearch.org/ark:/61903/1:1:VHCY-NLQ : 9 December 2014), Lee Angeloff, 05 Jul 1956; from "Montana Death Index, 1868-2011," database, Ancestry (http://www.ancestry.com : 2009); citing State of Montana Department of Public Health and Human Services, Office of Vital Statistics, Helena; "United States World War I Draft Registration Cards, 1917-1918," database with images, FamilySearch (https://familysearch.org/ark:/61903/1:1:K8QK-VL1 : 13 March 2018), Lee George Angeloff, 1917-1918; citing Yellowstone County, Montana, United States, NARA microfilm publication M1509 (Washington D.C.: National Archives and Records Administration, n.d.); FHL microfilm 1,711,531; "Find A Grave Index," database, FamilySearch (https://familysearch.org/ark:/61903/1:1:QV2F-NWY5 : 11 July 2016), Anna Kostova Angeloff, 1990; Burial, , Wheatland, Montana, United States of America, Harlowton Cemetery; citing record ID 68694238, Find a Grave, http://www.findagrave.com; "Anna K. Angeloff," The Billings Gazette (Billings, Montana) 17 Jul 1990, Page 6; "Lee Angeloff Laid to Rest," Eastern Montana Clarion (Ryegate, Montana) 12 Jul 1956, Page 1

[62] "Lee Angeloff Laid to Rest," Eastern Montana Clarion (Ryegate, Montana) 12 Jul 1956, Page 1; "Montana Flyer Killed in Crash," The Billings Gazette (Billings, Montana) 26 Aug 1947, Page 1

[63] "Mary Ann Lander," Great Falls Tribune (Great Falls, Montana) 20 Mar 1979, Page 5; "6 Applications are Received," The Billings Gazette (Billings, Montana) 28 Nov 1927, Page 3; https://www.findagrave.com/memorial/81056128/matrona-angeloff#view-photo=85666012; "United States, GenealogyBank Obituaries, 1980-2014," database with images, FamilySearch (https://familysearch.org/ark:/61903/1:1:QK55-1Y54 : accessed 31 December 2018), Nikol Angeloff in entry for Pete Angeloff, Montana, United States, 04 Jan 2011; from "Recent Newspaper Obituaries (1977 - Today)," database, GenealogyBank.com (http://www.genealogybank.com : 2014); citing Billings

Gazette, The, born-digital text; "Angeloff—Morris," The Billings Gazette (Billings, Montana) 14 May 1978, Page 66

[64] "Drowns in Yellowstone," The Missoulian (Missoula, Montana) 13 Aug 1922, Page 1; "Section Hand Drowned in Yellowstone," The Billings Gazette (Billings, Montana) 14 Aug 1922, Page 8

[65] "United States Census, 1940," database with images, FamilySearch (https://familysearch.org/ark:/61903/1:1:VB3Y-SVY : 15 March 2018), Naum Atenasoff, Ward 1, Miles City, School District 1 Miles City, Custer, Montana, United States; citing enumeration district (ED) 9-1, sheet 4B, line 46, family 88, Sixteenth Census of the United States, 1940, NARA digital publication T627. Records of the Bureau of the Census, 1790 - 2007, RG 29. Washington, D.C.: National Archives and Records Administration, 2012, roll 2216.; "Montana Death Index, 1860-2007," database, FamilySearch (https://familysearch.org/ark:/61903/1:1:VHCN-357 : 9 December 2014), Naum Atanasoff, 19 Jan 1960; from "Montana Death Index, 1868-2011," database, Ancestry (http://www.ancestry.com : 2009); citing State of Montana Department of Public Health and Human Services, Office of Vital Statistics, Helena.

https://www.findagrave.com/memorial/55764765; "Montana, County Marriages, 1865-1950," database with images, FamilySearch (https://familysearch.org/ark:/61903/1:1:F379-29Y : 25 September 2017), Naum Atanosoff and Harrietta Edith Green, 06 Feb 1929; citing Marriage, Miles City, Custer, Montana, various county courthouses, Montana; FHL microfilm 1,940,868. "United States Census, 1930," database with images, FamilySearch (https://familysearch.org/ark:/61903/1:1:XCMN-Y23 : accessed 29 December 2018), Naum Altanisff, Miles, Custer, Montana, United States; citing enumeration district (ED) ED 1, sheet 2A, line 42, family 48, NARA microfilm publication T626 (Washington D.C.: National Archives and Records Administration, 2002), roll 1254; FHL microfilm 2,340,989.

[66] "United States Census, 1920," database with images, FamilySearch (https://familysearch.org/ark:/61903/1:1:M8QQ-4F6 : accessed 28 December 2018), Dimitre Batchoff, Butte Ward 2a, Silver Bow, Montana, United States; citing ED 201, sheet 4B, line 76, family 74, NARA microfilm publication T625 (Washington D.C.: National Archives and Records Administration, 1992), roll 976; FHL microfilm 1,820,976.

[67] "Montana, County Births and Deaths, 1840-2004," database with images, FamilySearch (https://familysearch.org/ark:/61903/1:1:QKNR-CRC9 : 4 August 2017), Metody A Batchoff, 13 Jun 1932; citing Death, Butte, Silver Bow, Montana, United States, various county recorder offices; FHL microfilm 2,311,842.

[68] "United States Census, 1920," database with images, FamilySearch (https://familysearch.org/ark:/61903/1:1:M8QQ-4F6 : accessed 28 December 2018), Dimitre Batchoff, Butte Ward 2a, Silver Bow, Montana, United States; citing ED 201, sheet 4B, line 76, family 74, NARA microfilm publication T625

(Washington D.C.: National Archives and Records Administration, 1992), roll 976; FHL microfilm 1,820,976.

[69] "State and Federal Officials at Dinner Honoring D.A. Batchoff," The Montana Standard (Butte, Montana) 30 Apr 1949, Page 5

[70] "Summons," The Daily Missoulian (Missoula, Montana) 10 Nov 1911, Page 9

[71] "Batchoff to Take Up Duties as Rum Enforcement Chief," The Montana Standard (Butte, Montana) 21 Mar 1937, Page 1, 12

[72] "Summons," The Daily Missoulian (Missoula, Montana) 10 Nov 1911, Page 9

[73] "Sues for Damages," The Anaconda Standard (Anaconda, Montana) 11 Aug 1912, Page 11

[74] "Killing of Prokos and Trial of Papp," The Anaconda Standard (Anaconda, Montana) 09 May 1913, Page 9; "Bulgarians and Turks Mixed in Murder Case," The Anaconda Standard (Anaconda, Montana) 08 May 1913, Page 11.

[75] "Melzner Denies All of Batchoff's Claims," The Butte Miner (Butte, Montana) 27 Nov 1923, Page 6

[76] "Melzner is Winner in Batchoff Action," The Butte Miner (Butte, Montana) 06 Feb 1924, Page 6

[77] "Batchoff-Melzner Case Remittitur is Received," The Butte Miner (Butte, Montana) 13 Nov 1924, Page 14

[78] "United States Census, 1920," database with images, FamilySearch (https://familysearch.org/ark:/61903/1:1:M8QQ-4F6 : accessed 28 December 2018), Dimitre Batchoff, Butte Ward 2a, Silver Bow, Montana, United States; citing ED 201, sheet 4B, line 76, family 74, NARA microfilm publication T625 (Washington D.C.: National Archives and Records Administration, 1992), roll 976; FHL microfilm 1,820,976.

[79] "Deaths and Funerals," The Butte Miner (Butte, Montana) 16 Mar 1916, Page 6

[80] "Batchoff Assumes U.S. Marshal Post," The Independent-Record (Helena, Montana) 12 Jul 1934, Page 5

[81] "Montana, County Births and Deaths, 1840-2004," database with images, FamilySearch (https://familysearch.org/ark:/61903/1:1:QKNR-CRC9 : 4 August 2017), Metody A Batchoff, 13 Jun 1932; citing Death, Butte, Silver Bow, Montana, United States, various county recorder offices; FHL microfilm 2,311,842; "Batchoff Death," The Montana Standard (Butte, Montana) 14 Jun 1932, Page 5.

[82] "Metody A. Batchoff," The Montana Standard (Butte, Montana) 16 Jun 1932, Page 8

[83] "Batchoff Assumes U.S. Marshal Post," The Independent-Record (Helena, Montana) 12 Jul 1934, Page 5

[84] The Montana Standard (Butte, Montana) 03 Sep 1935, Page 5

[85] "Batchoff to Take Up Duties as Rum Enforcement Chief," The Montana Standard (Butte, Montana) 21 Mar 1937, Page 1, 12

[86] "Batchoff Says Bootlegging in State Nearly Wiped Out," The Independent-Record (Helena, Montana) 23 Oct 1938, Page 4

[87] "Batchoff Named Probation Officer," The Missoulian (Missoula, Montana) 30 Nov 1942, Page 8
[88] "Truman Names Batchoff as Marshal," The Independent-Record (Helena, Montana) 08 Mar 1949, Page 1
[89] "Federal Judge Lauds Batchoff's Record," The Montana Standard (Butte, Montana) 29 Oct 1953, Page 16
[90] "Mrs. Boris Batchoff Dies in Portland," The Montana Standard (Butte, Montana) 29 Jun 1962, Page 12
[91] "C.D. Botaff," The Daily Inter Lake (Kalispell, Montana) 31 Jan 1962, Page 3
[92] "United States World War I Draft Registration Cards, 1917-1918," database with images, FamilySearch (https://familysearch.org/ark:/61903/1:1:K8QN-DNQ : 13 March 2018), Christ Demetry Botaff, 1917-1918; citing Fergus County, Montana, United States, NARA microfilm publication M1509 (Washington D.C.: National Archives and Records Administration, n.d.); FHL microfilm 1,684,112.
[93] "C.D. Botaff," The Daily Inter Lake (Kalispell, Montana) 31 Jan 1962, Page 3
[94] "Botaff Appointed to Honorary Post," The Daily Inter Lake (Kalispell, Montana) 03 Apr 1959, Page 2
[95] "C.D. Botaff," The Daily Inter Lake (Kalispell, Montana) 31 Jan 1962, Page 3
[96] "Christ Botaff Dies in Whitefish," The Missoulian (Missoula, Montana) 26 Jan 1962, Page 8
[97] "Find A Grave Index," database, FamilySearch (https://familysearch.org/ark:/61903/1:1:QVLC-TH9N : 13 December 2015), Christ Demetry Botaff, 1962; Burial, Whitefish, Flathead, Montana, United States of America, Whitefish Cemetery; citing record ID 91751242, Find a Grave, http://www.findagrave.com.
[98] "United States World War I Draft Registration Cards, 1917-1918," database with images, FamilySearch (https://familysearch.org/ark:/61903/1:1:K8QN-1BR : 13 March 2018), Dino Buzenoff, 1917-1918; citing Missoula County, Montana, United States, NARA microfilm publication M1509 (Washington D.C.: National Archives and Records Administration, n.d.); FHL microfilm 1,711,435.
  https://www.findagrave.com/memorial/34914474; "Montana, Military Records, 1904-1918," database, FamilySearch (https://familysearch.org/ark:/61903/1:1:QP5T-5J4W : 2 November 2018), Dino Buzenoff, 11 Mar 1918; citing Military Service, Missoula, Montana, United States, Montana State Historical Society, Helena."United States Census, 1930," database with images, FamilySearch (https://familysearch.org/ark:/61903/1:1:XCMF-K4K : accessed 29 December 2018), Dino P Buzenoff in household of Hilman Korslund, Great Falls, Cascade, Montana, United States; citing enumeration district (ED) ED 8, sheet 11A, line 21, family 158, NARA microfilm publication T626 (Washington D.C.: National Archives and Records Administration, 2002), roll 1253; FHL microfilm 2,340,988.
[99] "Irwin Retires after 35 Years," The Daily Inter Lake (Kalispell, Montana) 24 Jun 1953, Page 6; "United States Census, 1940," database with images, FamilySearch

(https://familysearch.org/ark:/61903/1:1:VB31-N78 : 16 March 2018), James Christoff, Belton Township, Flathead, Montana, United States; citing enumeration district (ED) 15-1, sheet 3A, line 17, family 63, Sixteenth Census of the United States, 1940, NARA digital publication T627. Records of the Bureau of the Census, 1790 - 2007, RG 29. Washington, D.C.: National Archives and Records Administration, 2012, roll 2219; "United States Census, 1930," database with images, FamilySearch (https://familysearch.org/ark:/61903/1:1:XCM2-3WR : accessed 27 December 2018), James Christoff, Belton, Flathead, Montana, United States; citing enumeration district (ED) ED 2, sheet 3B, line 77, family 79, NARA microfilm publication T626 (Washington D.C.: National Archives and Records Administration, 2002), roll 1256; FHL microfilm 2,340,991; "United States World War I Draft Registration Cards, 1917-1918," database with images, FamilySearch (https://familysearch.org/ark:/61903/1:1:K8QJ-NX3 : 13 March 2018), James Christoff, 1917-1918; citing Phillips County, Montana, United States, NARA microfilm publication M1509 (Washington D.C.: National Archives and Records Administration, n.d.); FHL microfilm 1,711,438; "Montana, County Marriages, 1865-1950," database with images, FamilySearch (https://familysearch.org/ark:/61903/1:1:F33H-CM9 : 4 November 2017), James Christoff and Alice Alida Nelson, 29 Sep 1923; citing Marriage, Kalispell, Flathead, Montana, county courthouses, Montana; FHL microfilm 1,902,480; "Engagement Announced," The Missoulian (Missoula, Montana) 09 Apr 1944, Page 9; "Belton," The Daily Inter Lake (Kalispell, Montana) 12 Dec 1941, Page 10

[100] "United States Census, 1940," database with images, FamilySearch (https://familysearch.org/ark:/61903/1:1:VB3Y-762 : 15 March 2018), James Christhoff, Ward 1, Miles City, School District 1 Miles City, Custer, Montana, United States; citing enumeration district (ED) 9-1, sheet 1A, line 1, family 1, Sixteenth Census of the United States, 1940, NARA digital publication T627. Records of the Bureau of the Census, 1790 - 2007, RG 29. Washington, D.C.: National Archives and Records Administration, 2012, roll 2216.

"Montana, County Marriages, 1865-1950," database with images, FamilySearch (https://familysearch.org/ark:/61903/1:1:F3W1-58Z : 25 September 2017), James Christoff in entry for Tophal F. Grutkowski and Katherine L. Christoff, 12 Dec 1945; citing Marriage, Miles City, Custer, Montana, various county courthouses, Montana; FHL microfilm 1,940,870. "Jim Christoff," Great Falls Tribune (Great Falls, Montana) 16 Jan 1958, Page 6

[101] Theodore Christoff Dies at 99, Great Falls Tribune (Great Falls, Montana) 11 Nov 1971, Thu Page 8; Father Daughter Reunited After 53 Years Separation, Great Falls Tribune (Great Falls, Montana) 13 Jun 1958, Fri Page 11; Old Charlie Toasted on 99th Birthday, Great Falls Tribune (Great Falls, Montana) 26 Jan 1971, Tue Page 9; Father Daughter Reunited After 53 Years Separation, Great Falls Tribune (Great Falls, Montana) 13 Jun 1958, Fri Page 11

[102] "United States Census, 1920," database with images, FamilySearch (https://familysearch.org/ark:/61903/1:1:M83L-ZGK : accessed 30 December

2018), Vane Cotchoff in household of Ilio P Cotchoff, School District 169, Fergus, Montana, United States; citing ED 110, sheet 2B, line 64, family 60, NARA microfilm publication T625 (Washington D.C.: National Archives and Records Administration, 1992), roll 970; FHL microfilm 1,820,970.

[103] "United States Census, 1930," database with images, FamilySearch (https://familysearch.org/ark:/61903/1:1:XCMV-8JJ : accessed 30 December 2018), Alex Demitroff, Warm Springs, Deer Lodge, Montana, United States; citing enumeration district (ED) ED 4, sheet 5B, line 87, family , NARA microfilm publication T626 (Washington D.C.: National Archives and Records Administration, 2002), roll 1255; FHL microfilm 2,340,990; "Two Committed to Asylum," The Butte Daily Post (Butte, Montana) 26 Oct 1908, Page 4; "United States Census, 1910," database with images, FamilySearch (https://familysearch.org/ark:/61903/1:1:MLCQ-93G : accessed 31 December 2018), Alex Demitroff, Warm Springs School District, Deer Lodge, Montana, United States; citing enumeration district (ED) ED 8, sheet 16A, family 120, NARA microfilm publication T624 (Washington D.C.: National Archives and Records Administration, 1982), roll 831; FHL microfilm 1,374,844; "United States Census, 1920," database with images, FamilySearch (https://familysearch.org/ark:/61903/1:1:M83K-ZLP : accessed 31 December 2018), Alex Dimitroff, Warm Springs, Deer Lodge, Montana, United States; citing ED 20, sheet 4B, line 82, family 317, NARA microfilm publication T625 (Washington D.C.: National Archives and Records Administration, 1992), roll 969; FHL microfilm 1,820,969.https://www.findagrave.com/memorial/184217427

[104] "United States Census, 1920," database with images, FamilySearch (https://familysearch.org/ark:/61903/1:1:M83K-C3L : accessed 27 December 2018), George Dimitroff in household of Nome Tarpo, Miles Ward 1, Custer, Montana, United States; citing ED 36, sheet 8A, line 43, family 178, NARA microfilm publication T625 (Washington D.C.: National Archives and Records Administration, 1992), roll 969; FHL microfilm 1,820,969; "Find A Grave Index," database, FamilySearch (https://familysearch.org/ark:/61903/1:1:Q2S9-18HN : 15 March 2016), George Dimitroff, 1969; Burial, Butte, Silver Bow, Montana, United States of America, Mountain View Cemetery; citing record ID 153926311, Find a Grave, http://www.findagrave.com; "United States World War I Draft Registration Cards, 1917-1918," database with images, FamilySearch (https://familysearch.org/ark:/61903/1:1:K8QF-2QS : 13 March 2018), George Dimitroff, 1917-1918; citing Custer County, Montana, United States, NARA microfilm publication M1509 (Washington D.C.: National Archives and Records Administration, n.d.); FHL microfilm 1,684,108; "Montana, County Births and Deaths, 1840-2004," database with images, FamilySearch (https://familysearch.org/ark:/61903/1:1:QKNR-F3BG : 4 August 2017), George Dimitroff, 08 Feb 1969; citing Death, Butte, Silver Bow, Montana, United States, various county recorder offices; FHL microfilm 2,312,205; "Montana, Military Records, 1904-1918," database, FamilySearch

(https://familysearch.org/ark:/61903/1:1:QP2H-KNKN : 2 November 2018), George Dimitroff, 25 Apr 1918; citing Military Service, Custer, Montana, United States, Montana State Historical Society, Helena. "George Dimitroff Dies in Hospital," The Montana Standard (Butte, Montana) 09 Feb 1969, Sun Page 16

[105] "Dimitroff Hurled Off Hand Car," The Butte Daily Post (Butte, Montana) 23 Jul 1912, Page 7

[106] The Anaconda Standard (Anaconda, Montana) 15 Aug 1912, Thu Page 8

[107] "United States Census, 1930," database with images, FamilySearch (https://familysearch.org/ark:/61903/1:1:XCMB-WCD : accessed 28 December 2018), John Dimitroff, Cottonwood, Powell, Montana, United States; citing enumeration district (ED) ED 5, sheet 5A, line 30, family 120, NARA microfilm publication T626 (Washington D.C.: National Archives and Records Administration, 2002), roll 1260; FHL microfilm 2,340,995; "John Dimitroff," Great Falls Tribune (Great Falls, Montana) 22 Jul 1934, Page 11; "Railway Employee is Shot to Death; Suicide Indicated," Great Falls Tribune (Great Falls, Montana) 20 Jul 1934, Page 16

[108] "Tudor Dimitroff Rites Monday," The Montana Standard (Butte, Montana) 02 Feb 1958, Page 28

[109] "United States World War I Draft Registration Cards, 1917-1918," database with images, FamilySearch (https://familysearch.org/ark:/61903/1:1:K8QJ-MVX : 13 March 2018), Alex Profe Dimzoff, 1917-1918; citing Missoula County, Montana, United States, NARA microfilm publication M1509 (Washington D.C.: National Archives and Records Administration, n.d.); FHL microfilm 1,711,436; "United States Census, 1940," database with images, FamilySearch (https://familysearch.org/ark:/61903/1:1:VB3T-WM8 : 15 March 2018), Alex Dimzoff in household of Laura M Parent, Ward 4, Great Falls, School District 1 Great Falls, Cascade, Montana, United States; citing enumeration district (ED) 7-21A, sheet 7B, line 64, family 152, Sixteenth Census of the United States, 1940, NARA digital publication T627. Records of the Bureau of the Census, 1790 - 2007, RG 29. Washington, D.C.: National Archives and Records Administration, 2012, roll 2214; "Find A Grave Index," database, FamilySearch (https://familysearch.org/ark:/61903/1:1:QVKL-BW96 : 13 December 2015), Alex P Dimzoff, 1948; Burial, Great Falls, Cascade, Montana, United States of America, Highland Cemetery; citing record ID 47845724, Find a Grave, http://www.findagrave.com.

[110] "United States World War I Draft Registration Cards, 1917-1918," database with images, FamilySearch (https://familysearch.org/ark:/61903/1:1:K8QJ-M2F : 13 March 2018), Clem Profa Dimsoff, 1917-1918; citing Missoula County, Montana, United States, NARA microfilm publication M1509 (Washington D.C.: National Archives and Records Administration, n.d.); FHL microfilm 1,711,436.
"United States Census, 1920," database with images, FamilySearch (https://familysearch.org/ark:/61903/1:1:M83T-QTC : accessed 27 December 2018), Clem Dimzoff, School District 9, Lewis and Clark, Montana, United States;

citing ED 115, sheet 10B, line 84, family 235, NARA microfilm publication T625 (Washington D.C.: National Archives and Records Administration, 1992), roll 972; FHL microfilm 1,820,972; "United States Census, 1930," database with images, FamilySearch (https://familysearch.org/ark:/61903/1:1:XCMF-T68 : accessed 27 December 2018), Clem P Dimzoff, Great Falls, Cascade, Montana, United States; citing enumeration district (ED) ED 17, sheet 1B, line 59, family 19, NARA microfilm publication T626 (Washington D.C.: National Archives and Records Administration, 2002), roll 1253; FHL microfilm 2,340,988; "Montana, County Births and Deaths, 1840-2004," database with images, FamilySearch (https://familysearch.org/ark:/61903/1:1:QKNR-25VB : 4 August 2017), Clem Dimzoff in entry for Vernell, 26 Dec 1918; citing Birth, East Helena, Lewis And Clark, Montana, United States, various county recorder offices; FHL microfilm 2,314,612; https://www.findagrave.com/memorial/46223153/clime-p-dimzoff

"Washington, County Marriages, 1855-2008," database with images, FamilySearch (https://familysearch.org/ark:/61903/1:1:QPMJ-4971 : 28 November 2018), Clime P Dimzoff and Violet Smith, 14 Feb 1945, King, Washington, United States, State Archives, Olympia; FamilySearch digital folder 004197546; "Clime Dimzoff Dies at Hospital", Great Falls Tribune (Great Falls, Montana); 16 Mar 1949, Page 8 "Scaffold Breaks, Plasterer Hurt," The Independent-Record (Helena, Montana) 27 Jul 1928, Page 6

[111]"Assault Charge Filed," Great Falls Tribune (Great Falls, Montana) 03 Mar 1932, Page 6; "Worker Confined for 25 Days When He Defaults Fine," Great Falls Tribune (Great Falls, Montana) 05 Mar 1933, Page 11; "Mrs. Dimzoff Files Action for Divorce," Great Falls Tribune (Great Falls, Montana) 17 Aug 1933, Page 12; "Husband Contents Wife's Demand for Separation Decree," Great Falls Tribune (Great Falls, Montana) 30 Sep 1933, Page 7 "Husband Contents Wife's Demand for Separation Decree," Great Falls Tribune (Great Falls, Montana) 30 Sep 1933, Page 7 "Mrs. Lula Dimzoff Granted Divorce," Great Falls Tribune (Great Falls, Montana) 19 Jan 1934, Page 9

[112] "Rigged Wedding Goes 50 Years," The Montana Standard (Butte, Montana) 19 Sep 1971, Page 20

[113]"United States Census, 1940," database with images, FamilySearch (https://familysearch.org/ark:/61903/1:1:VBQ7-G84 : 15 March 2018), Olga Eloff in household of Blage Eloff, Superior Township, Mineral, Montana, United States; citing enumeration district (ED) 31-6, sheet 13A, line 5, family 298, Sixteenth Census of the United States, 1940, NARA digital publication T627. Records of the Bureau of the Census, 1790 - 2007, RG 29. Washington, D.C.: National Archives and Records Administration, 2012, roll 2225; "Montana, County Marriages, 1865-1950," database with images, FamilySearch (https://familysearch.org/ark:/61903/1:1:F3WP-QTG : 4 November 2017), William O. Webster and Olga Eloff, 05 Sep 1949; citing Marriage, Missoula, Missoula, Montana, various county courthouses, Montana; FHL microfilm 1,889,006; "Montana, County Marriages, 1865-1950," database with images,

FamilySearch (https://familysearch.org/ark:/61903/1:1:F3QX-CQV : 25 September 2017), Blago Eloff and Para Taleva, 11 Sep 1921; citing Marriage, Lewistown, Fergus, Montana, various county courthouses, Montana; FHL microfilm 1,941,298.

[114] "Gordon's Men Arrest Eight for Gambling," Great Falls Tribune (Great Falls, Montana) 23 Jan 1921, Page 11

[115] "Deputies Raid Coffee House," Great Falls Tribune (Great Falls, Montana) 23 Sep 1921, Page 5

[116] "Montana, Cascade County Records, 1880-2009," database with images, FamilySearch (https://familysearch.org/ark:/61903/1:1:QKM7-MQ36 : 4 August 2017), Blage Eloff in entry for MM9.1.1/QKM7-MQ3D:, ; citing Death, newspaper, volume date range Eggler-Ernst, 1880-2002, Great Falls Genealogy Society.

[117] "Safety Record for Rail Man," The Missoulian (Missoula, Montana) 18 Jul 1942, Page 2

[118] "Montana, Cascade County Records, 1880-2009," database with images, FamilySearch (https://familysearch.org/ark:/61903/1:1:QKM7-MQ36 : 4 August 2017), Blage Eloff in entry for MM9.1.1/QKM7-MQ3D:, ; citing Death, newspaper, volume date range Eggler-Ernst, 1880-2002, Great Falls Genealogy Society.

[119] "Awarded Air Medal," The Missoulian (Missoula, Montana) 25 Feb 1945, Page 9

[120] "James Eloff Sr.," Great Falls Tribune (Great Falls, Montana) 05 Jun 1998, Page 8

[121] "Alex N. Taleff," Great Falls Tribune (Great Falls, Montana) 25 May 2011, Page 12

[122] "George N. Taleff," Great Falls Tribune (Great Falls, Montana) 30 Apr 2000, Page 14

[123] "Rollins Wins G.F. Electrics' Taleff Award," Great Falls Tribune (Great Falls, Montana) 29 Dec 1975, Page 15

[124] Great Falls Tribune (Great Falls, Montana) 16 May 1976, Page 15

[125] "Daniel Evans Dies at 74 in Lewistown," Great Falls Tribune (Great Falls, Montana) 14 Jan 1970, Page 12; "United States Census, 1940," database with images, FamilySearch (https://familysearch.org/ark:/61903/1:1:VB3R-HLP : 15 March 2018), Diamond Evans in household of Bill Massas, Ward 2, Great Falls, School District 1 Great Falls, Cascade, Montana, United States; citing enumeration district (ED) 7-7, sheet 64B, line 77, family 37, Sixteenth Census of the United States, 1940, NARA digital publication T627. Records of the Bureau of the Census, 1790 - 2007, RG 29. Washington, D.C.: National Archives and Records Administration, 2012, roll 2214.

[126] "Gamell Rites Saturday," Great Falls Tribune (Great Falls, Montana) 29 Jan 1943, Page 12; United States Census, 1940," database with images, FamilySearch (https://familysearch.org/ark:/61903/1:1:VB31-8KS : 16 March 2018), Saltona Gamell in household of John Gamell, Denton, School District 84 Denton, Fergus, Montana, United States; citing enumeration district (ED) 14-58, sheet 4A, line 2,

family 68, Sixteenth Census of the United States, 1940, NARA digital publication T627. Records of the Bureau of the Census, 1790 - 2007, RG 29. Washington, D.C.: National Archives and Records Administration, 2012, roll 2218; "Montana, Cascade County Records, 1880-2009," database with images, FamilySearch (https://familysearch.org/ark:/61903/1:1:QKM7-9VYN : 4 August 2017), John Gamell, 01 Oct 1980; citing Death, Great Falls Tribune newspaper, volume date range Freedle-Gardner, 1880-2002, Great Falls Genealogy Society; "Find A Grave Index," database, FamilySearch (https://familysearch.org/ark:/61903/1:1:QV2P-8DYV : 13 December 2015), John Gamell, 1980; Burial, Lewistown, Fergus, Montana, United States of America, Lewistown City Cemetery; citing record ID 77131706, Find a Grave, http://www.findagrave.com; "Montana, Chouteau County Records,1876-2011," database with images, FamilySearch (https://familysearch.org/ark:/61903/1:1:QJDL-ZDDY : 24 May 2014), John Gamell in entry for null, Birth, 12 Sep 1921, Geraldine, Chouteau, Montana, United States; citing vol. Birth certificates no 2601-2850, cert. #2632, various offices Chouteau County Courthouse and Museum of the Northern Plains River and Plains Society, Fort Benton; FamilySearch digital folder 005629113; "Lewistown – Gamell, John," Great Falls Tribune (Great Falls, Montana) 01 Oct 1980, Page 42; "Daniel Evans Dies at 74 In Lewistown," Great Falls Tribune (Great Falls, Montana) 14 Jan 1970, Page 12; "Six Fergus County Persons Naturalized," Great Falls Tribune (Great Falls, Montana) 27 Sep 1940, Page 9; "Denton Resident Dies at Lewistown Hospital," Great Falls Tribune (Great Falls, Montana) 28 Jan 1943, Page 10

[127] "United States Census, 1930," database with images, FamilySearch (https://familysearch.org/ark:/61903/1:1:XCMB-KP2 : accessed 28 December 2018), Nicklas Ginoff, Lincoln, Powell, Montana, United States; citing enumeration district (ED) ED 9, sheet 4B, line 73, family 79, NARA microfilm publication T626 (Washington D.C.: National Archives and Records Administration, 2002), roll 1260; FHL microfilm 2,340,995; "United States Census, 1940," database with images, FamilySearch (https://familysearch.org/ark:/61903/1:1:VBQH-YZL : 15 March 2018), Nick E Ginoff, Helmville, Lincoln Township, Powell, Montana, United States; citing enumeration district (ED) 39-9, sheet 5A, line 3, family 99, Sixteenth Census of the United States, 1940, NARA digital publication T627. Records of the Bureau of the Census, 1790 - 2007, RG 29. Washington, D.C.: National Archives and Records Administration, 2012, roll 2227; "United States Census, 1920," database with images, FamilySearch (https://familysearch.org/ark:/61903/1:1:M8Q9-SR3 : accessed 28 December 2018), Nicholas E Ginoff, Lincoln, Powell, Montana, United States; citing ED 176, sheet 4A, line 1, family 71, NARA microfilm publication T625 (Washington D.C.: National Archives and Records Administration, 1992), roll 974; FHL microfilm 1,820,974; https://www.findagrave.com/memorial/152041871

"United States World War I Draft Registration Cards, 1917-1918," database with images, FamilySearch (https://familysearch.org/ark:/61903/1:1:K8QJ-26H : 13 March 2018), Nick Evan Ginoff, 1917-1918; citing Powell County, Montana, United States, NARA microfilm publication M1509 (Washington D.C.: National Archives and Records Administration, n.d.); FHL microfilm 1,711,439; "United States, Veterans Administration Master Index, 1917-1940," database, FamilySearch (https://familysearch.org/ark:/61903/1:1:Q5F8-D5W2 : 5 December 2018), Nick E Ginoff, 20 Nov 1917; citing Military Service, NARA microfilm publication 76193916 (St. Louis: National Archives and Records Administration, 1985), various roll numbers; "Montana Death Index, 1860-2007," database, FamilySearch (https://familysearch.org/ark:/61903/1:1:VHCP-C8V : 9 December 2014), Thomas Ginoff, 20 Apr 1924; from "Montana Death Index, 1868-2011," database, Ancestry (http://www.ancestry.com : 2009); citing State of Montana Department of Public Health and Human Services, Office of Vital Statistics, Helena; "Seeking Office," The Montana Standard (Butte, Montana)17 Jun 1938, Page 7; "Ginoff and Pike Attend Meeting," The Missoulian (Missoula, Montana) 10 May 1953, Page 28; "Blackfoot Telephone Co-op is Near Incorporation Stage," The Missoulian (Missoula, Montana) 06 Mar 1954, Page 10

[128] "United States Census, 1930," database with images, FamilySearch (https://familysearch.org/ark:/61903/1:1:XCMB-KP2 : accessed 28 December 2018), Nicklas Ginoff, Lincoln, Powell, Montana, United States; citing enumeration district (ED) ED 9, sheet 4B, line 73, family 79, NARA microfilm publication T626 (Washington D.C.: National Archives and Records Administration, 2002), roll 1260; FHL microfilm 2,340,995. "Prospects Seen For Good Crops," The Missoulian (Missoula, Montana) 26 Aug 1948, Page 2; "Peter Evan Ginoff," The Missoulian (Missoula, Montana) 23 Feb 1987, Page 12

[129] "Nurmi George," The Missoulian (Missoula, Montana) 05 Jan 1941, Page 4; "Nurmi George is Taken by Death at Ranch Cabin," The Missoulian (Missoula, Montana) 02 Jan 1941, Page 6

[130] "United States Census, 1930," database with images, FamilySearch (https://familysearch.org/ark:/61903/1:1:XC9S-W6V : accessed 28 December 2018), Van Janoff, Butte, Silver Bow, Montana, United States; citing enumeration district (ED) ED 42, sheet 6B, line 2, family 170, NARA microfilm publication T626 (Washington D.C.: National Archives and Records Administration, 2002), roll 1262; FHL microfilm 2,340,997.

"United States Census, 1940," database with images, FamilySearch (https://familysearch.org/ark:/61903/1:1:VBQD-5RT : 16 March 2018), Van Janeff, Ward 8, Butte, Election Precinct 48, Silver Bow, Montana, United States; citing enumeration district (ED) 47-42, sheet 6A, line 4, family 155, Sixteenth Census of the United States, 1940, NARA digital publication T627. Records of the Bureau of the Census, 1790 - 2007, RG 29. Washington, D.C.: National Archives and Records Administration, 2012, roll 2231.

https://www.findagrave.com/memorial/167113576

"Montana, County Marriages, 1865-1950," database with images, FamilySearch (https://familysearch.org/ark:/61903/1:1:F3WT-TV9 : 21 September 2017), Van Janeff and Irene Elizabeth Shaffer, 21 Aug 1927; citing Marriage, Silver Bow, , Montana, various county courthouses, Montana; FHL microfilm 1,939,681.

"United States World War I Draft Registration Cards, 1917-1918," database with images, FamilySearch (https://familysearch.org/ark:/61903/1:1:K8QX-7ZY : 13 March 2018), Van Janeff, 1917-1918; citing Butte City, Montana, United States, NARA microfilm publication M1509 (Washington D.C.: National Archives and Records Administration, n.d.); FHL microfilm 1,684,102.

"Montana, County Births and Deaths, 1840-2004," database with images, FamilySearch (https://familysearch.org/ark:/61903/1:1:QKNR-XZPZ : 4 August 2017), Van Janeff, 05 Apr 1973; citing Death, Balen, Deer Lodge, Montana, United States, various county recorder offices; FHL microfilm 2,312,185. "Van Janeff, 75," The Montana Standard (Butte, Montana) 07 Apr 1973, Page 2

[131] "John Kostoff Dies," The Montana Standard (Butte, Montana) 15 Jan 1936, Page 3

[132] "Louis Kostoff, 69, Called by Death," The Montana Standard (Butte, Montana) 04 Feb 1960, Page 10; "United States Census, 1930," database with images, FamilySearch (https://familysearch.org/ark:/61903/1:1:XCMB-QNB : accessed 29 December 2018), Lewis Kostoff, Deer Lodge, Powell, Montana, United States; citing enumeration district (ED) ED 4, sheet 4A, line 41, family , NARA microfilm publication T626 (Washington D.C.: National Archives and Records Administration, 2002), roll 1260; FHL microfilm 2,340,995.

[133] "United States Census, 1920," database with images, FamilySearch (https://familysearch.org/ark:/61903/1:1:M83K-QBN : accessed 28 December 2018), John Kosty, Miles Ward 3, Custer, Montana, United States; citing ED 41, sheet 20A, line 20, family 27, NARA microfilm publication T625 (Washington D.C.: National Archives and Records Administration, 1992), roll 969; FHL microfilm 1,820,969.

[134]"United States Census, 1940," database with images, FamilySearch (https://familysearch.org/ark:/61903/1:1:VBQM-K3S : 16 March 2018), Alexander Ladinoff, Whitefish Township, Flathead, Montana, United States; citing enumeration district (ED) 15-34, sheet 4B, line 49, family 85, Sixteenth Census of the United States, 1940, NARA digital publication T627. Records of the Bureau of the Census, 1790 - 2007, RG 29. Washington, D.C.: National Archives and Records Administration, 2012, roll 2219; "Find A Grave Index," database, FamilySearch (https://familysearch.org/ark:/61903/1:1:QVLC-TCSM : 13 December 2015), Alexander D Lodinoff, 1952; Burial, Whitefish, Flathead, Montana, United States of America, Whitefish Cemetery; citing record ID 91750969, Find a Grave, http://www.findagrave.com.

https://www.findagrave.com/memorial/162583795/madeline-anderson;

"Alexander Lodinoff", Great Falls Tribune (Great Falls, Montana) 14 Nov 1952, Fri Page 4

[135] "Works at Essex," Great Falls Tribune (Great Falls, Montana) 01 Mar 1940, Page 4; "Service Discharges," The Daily Inter Lake (Kalispell, Montana) 26 Jun 1946, Page 8; "Service Discharges," The Daily Inter Lake (Kalispell, Montana) 06 Sep 1946, Page 4; "Havre Vets Offer Help in Defense," Great Falls Tribune (Great Falls, Montana) 07 Feb 1951, Page 4; "Marriage Licenses," Great Falls Tribune (Great Falls, Montana) 02 Feb 1952, Page 7; "Lodinoff Named to VFW Office," The Havre Daily News (Havre, Montana) 29 Nov 1968, Page 2 "Obituaries," Great Falls Tribune (Great Falls, Montana) 10 Dec 2002, Page 8

[136] "United States Census, 1940," database with images, FamilySearch (https://familysearch.org/ark:/61903/1:1:VB3Y-V7Y : 15 March 2018), Nick Lazoff, School District 3 Kircher, Custer, Montana, United States; citing enumeration district (ED) 9-12, sheet 1B, line 75, family 19, Sixteenth Census of the United States, 1940, NARA digital publication T627. Records of the Bureau of the Census, 1790 - 2007, RG 29. Washington, D.C.: National Archives and Records Administration, 2012, roll 2216; "Montana, County Marriages, 1865-1950," database with images, FamilySearch (https://familysearch.org/ark:/61903/1:1:F37S-MHL : 25 September 2017), Nick Lazoff and Stella Zawada, 05 Apr 1934; citing Marriage, Miles City, Custer, Montana, county courthouses, Montana; FHL microfilm 1,940,868; "Montana Death Index, 1860-2007," database, FamilySearch (https://familysearch.org/ark:/61903/1:1:VHC1-Z2K : 9 December 2014), Nick Lazoff, 21 Aug 1972; from "Montana Death Index, 1868-2011," database, Ancestry (http://www.ancestry.com : 2009); citing State of Montana Department of Public Health and Human Services, Office of Vital Statistics, Helena; "Lawrence Nick Lazoff," The Billings Gazette (Billings, Montana) 19 Feb 1997, Page 11

[137] "United States Census, 1940," database with images, FamilySearch (https://familysearch.org/ark:/61903/1:1:VBQ8-25S : 16 March 2018), George Demitroff in household of Louis Luchis, Ward 3, Butte, Election Precinct 15, Silver Bow, Montana, United States; citing enumeration district (ED) 47-16, sheet 12A, line 28, family 292, Sixteenth Census of the United States, 1940, NARA digital publication T627. Records of the Bureau of the Census, 1790 - 2007, RG 29. Washington, D.C.: National Archives and Records Administration, 2012, roll 2230; "Louis Lushia, 73, Ex-Miner, Dies,"  Montana Standard-Post (Butte, Montana) 26 Apr 1966,  Page 5

[138] "George Makedonski Is Seeking Damages for Loss of Trunk," The Butte Daily Post (Butte, Montana) 02 Jul 1910, Sat Page 4

[139] "He Loses His Satchel Wants the Road to Pay," The Anaconda Standard (Anaconda, Montana) 03 Jul 1910, Page 10

[140] "Makedonski Gets Damagers," The Butte Daily Post (Butte, Montana) 06 Jul 1910, Page 5

[141] "United States Census, 1940," database with images, FamilySearch (https://familysearch.org/ark:/61903/1:1:VBQ8-DXQ : 16 March 2018), Theodore Mano in household of Samuel Stanisich, Ward 1, Butte, Election Precinct 11,

Silver Bow, Montana, United States; citing enumeration district (ED) 47-9, sheet 8A, line 24, family 188, Sixteenth Census of the United States, 1940, NARA digital publication T627. Records of the Bureau of the Census, 1790 - 2007, RG 29. Washington, D.C.: National Archives and Records Administration, 2012, roll 2230.
[142] "Theodore Mano," The Montana Standard (Butte, Montana) 23 Sep 1949, Page 5
[143] "United States Census, 1930," database with images, FamilySearch (https://familysearch.org/ark:/61903/1:1:XCMG-TTL : accessed 28 December 2018), Paul Mike, Hobson, Judith Basin, Montana, United States; citing enumeration district (ED) ED 23, sheet 3A, line 7, family 58, NARA microfilm publication T626 (Washington D.C.: National Archives and Records Administration, 2002), roll 1257; FHL microfilm 2,340,992; "United States Census, 1940," database with images, FamilySearch (https://familysearch.org/ark:/61903/1:1:VBQJ-9CS : 13 March 2018), Paul Mike, Broadview, School District 21 Broadview, Yellowstone, Montana, United States; citing enumeration district (ED) 56-31, sheet 2B, line 50, family 41, Sixteenth Census of the United States, 1940, NARA digital publication T627. Records of the Bureau of the Census, 1790 - 2007, RG 29. Washington, D.C.: National Archives and Records Administration, 2012, roll 2234;
https://www.findagrave.com/memorial/91792897#view-photo=135565561
"United States World War I Draft Registration Cards, 1917-1918," database with images, FamilySearch (https://familysearch.org/ark:/61903/1:1:K8QK-RNR : 13 March 2018), Paul Mike, 1917-1918; citing Yellowstone County, Montana, United States, NARA microfilm publication M1509 (Washington D.C.: National Archives and Records Administration, n.d.); FHL microfilm 1,711,532; "Montana, County Marriages, 1865-1950," database with images, FamilySearch (https://familysearch.org/ark:/61903/1:1:F37M-12S : 25 September 2017), Paul Mike in entry for William K. Shamanoff and Katherine Mike, 10 Mar 1930; citing Marriage, Great Falls, Cascade, Montana, various county courthouses, Montana; FHL microfilm 1,940,170; "United States Census, 1940," database with images, FamilySearch (https://familysearch.org/ark:/61903/1:1:VBQM-VJ1 : 14 March 2018), William R Shamanoff, Bozeman, Election Precinct 3, Gallatin, Montana, United States; citing enumeration district (ED) 16-3, sheet 1A, line 17, family 10, Sixteenth Census of the United States, 1940, NARA digital publication T627. Records of the Bureau of the Census, 1790 - 2007, RG 29. Washington, D.C.: National Archives and Records Administration, 2012, roll 2220;
https://www.findagrave.com/memorial/91796870
[144] https://www.findagrave.com/memorial/22577992/patricia-anne-rowley
[145] "United States Census, 1940," database with images, FamilySearch (https://familysearch.org/ark:/61903/1:1:VBQX-BV9 : 13 March 2018), K Lazar Nanoff, School District 2 Frazer, Valley, Montana, United States; citing enumeration district (ED) 53-8, sheet 3B, line 42, family 42, Sixteenth Census of the United States, 1940, NARA digital publication T627. Records of the Bureau of

the Census, 1790 - 2007, RG 29. Washington, D.C.: National Archives and Records Administration, 2012, roll 2233; "United States World War I Draft Registration Cards, 1917-1918," database with images, FamilySearch (https://familysearch.org/ark:/61903/1:1:K689-FTY : 13 March 2018), Lazar Kostoff Nanoff, 1917-1918; citing Corson County, South Dakota, United States, NARA microfilm publication M1509 (Washington D.C.: National Archives and Records Administration, n.d.); FHL microfilm 1,877,789; "United States Census, 1920," database with images, FamilySearch (https://familysearch.org/ark:/61903/1:1:M6JZ-M4S : accessed 27 December 2018), Lazar K Nanoff, Township 20, Corson, South Dakota, United States; citing ED 31, sheet 2B, line 61, family 41, NARA microfilm publication T625 (Washington D.C.: National Archives and Records Administration, 1992), roll 1716; FHL microfilm 1,821,716; "Find A Grave Index," database, FamilySearch (https://familysearch.org/ark:/61903/1:1:Q2S9-1JDQ : 15 March 2016), Lazar K Nanoff, 1953; Burial, Glasgow, Valley, Montana, United States of America, Highland Cemetery; citing record ID 157044512, Find a Grave, http://www.findagrave.com;

[146] "United States World War I Draft Registration Cards, 1917-1918," database with images, FamilySearch (https://familysearch.org/ark:/61903/1:1:K8Q6-PFP : 13 March 2018), Noso Naumoff, 1917-1918; citing Blaine County, Montana, United States, NARA microfilm publication M1509 (Washington D.C.: National Archives and Records Administration, n.d.); FHL microfilm 1,684,100.

[147] "Sues for Injuries," The Montana Standard (Butte, Montana) 11 Oct 1932, Page 5

[148] "Ruling is Entered on Damage Action by Railway Worker," Great Falls Tribune (Great Falls, Montana) 06 May 1933, Page 10

[149] "United States Census, 1940," database with images, FamilySearch (https://familysearch.org/ark:/61903/1:1:VBQZ-D7Y : 15 March 2018), George Nickoloff, Brockton, School District 55, Roosevelt, Montana, United States; citing enumeration district (ED) 43-28, sheet 5B, line 42, family 95, Sixteenth Census of the United States, 1940, NARA digital publication T627. Records of the Bureau of the Census, 1790 - 2007, RG 29. Washington, D.C.: National Archives and Records Administration, 2012, roll 2228; "United States Census, 1930," database with images, FamilySearch (https://familysearch.org/ark:/61903/1:1:XCM1-G6Z : accessed 28 December 2018), George Nickoloff, School District 55, Roosevelt, Montana, United States; citing enumeration district (ED) ED 28, sheet 3A, line 38, family 44, NARA microfilm publication T626 (Washington D.C.: National Archives and Records Administration, 2002), roll 1261; FHL microfilm 2,340,996; "United States Census, 1920," database with images, FamilySearch (https://familysearch.org/ark:/61903/1:1:M8QS-TJ7 : accessed 28 December 2018), George Nickoloff, School District 55, Roosevelt, Montana, United States; citing ED 195, sheet 3A, line 13, family 71, NARA microfilm publication T625 (Washington D.C.: National Archives and Records Administration, 1992), roll 975;

FHL microfilm 1,820,975; "Montana Death Index, 1860-2007," database, FamilySearch (https://familysearch.org/ark:/61903/1:1:VHCJ-WRW : 9 December 2014), George Nickoloff, 25 Apr 1969; from "Montana Death Index, 1868-2011," database, Ancestry (http://www.ancestry.com : 2009); citing State of Montana Department of Public Health and Human Services, Office of Vital Statistics, Helena; "Treasure State Deaths," Great Falls Tribune (Great Falls, Montana) 28 Apr 1969, Mon Page 4; "Veteran Section Foreman Retires After 47 Years of Service," Great Falls Tribune (Great Falls, Montana) 04 Jan 1959, Page 38; "After 48 Years in States, She's Finally a Citizen," The Billings Gazette (Billings, Montana) 20 Sep 1978, Page 17 "Area Deaths," The Billings Gazette (Billings, Montana) 28 Feb 1993, Page 4

[150] "Brockton Soldier Wins Promotion in Korea," Great Falls Tribune (Great Falls, Montana) 01 Nov 1953, Page 59

[151] "2 Receive Doctorates," The Billings Gazette (Billings, Montana) 11 Oct 1975, Page 10

[152] "EMC Professors Honored by Scholarship Foundation," The Billings Gazette (Billings, Montana) 02 May 1985, Page 15

[153] "United States Census, 1940," database with images, FamilySearch (https://familysearch.org/ark:/61903/1:1:VBQH-3ZY : 15 March 2018), Louis Phillips, School District 18 Valier, Pondera, Montana, United States; citing enumeration district (ED) 37-16, sheet 1A, line 13, family 3, Sixteenth Census of the United States, 1940, NARA digital publication T627. Records of the Bureau of the Census, 1790 - 2007, RG 29. Washington, D.C.: National Archives and Records Administration, 2012, roll 2227; "United States Census, 1930," database with images, FamilySearch (https://familysearch.org/ark:/61903/1:1:XCMY-G1Z : accessed 28 December 2018), Louis Phillips, Valier, Pondera, Montana, United States; citing enumeration district (ED) ED 15, sheet 2B, line 62, family 39, NARA microfilm publication T626 (Washington D.C.: National Archives and Records Administration, 2002), roll 1260; FHL microfilm 2,340,995; "Montana, Military Records, 1904-1918," database, FamilySearch (https://familysearch.org/ark:/61903/1:1:QP5L-LKJV : 2 November 2018), Louis Phillips, 25 Jul 1918; citing Military Service, Choteau, Teton, Montana, United States, Montana State Historical Society, Helena; https://www.findagrave.com/memorial/24696597
  https://www.findagrave.com/memorial/24696173/blanch-ruth-phillips; https://www.findagrave.com/memorial/24696394/c_-f_-phillips; "Montana, County Marriages, 1865-1950," database with images, FamilySearch (https://familysearch.org/ark:/61903/1:1:F3QR-SXS : 10 February 2018), Louis Phillips and Blanche Ruth Hartwell, 07 Nov 1919; citing Marriage, Great Falls, Cascade, Montana, various county courthouses, Montana; FHL microfilm 1,940,168."Montana, County Marriages, 1865-1950," database with images, FamilySearch (https://familysearch.org/ark:/61903/1:1:F3WM-5Q4 : 7 December 2014), Edward Louis Phillips and Betty Jane Fowler, 09 Aug 1942; citing Marriage,

Cut Bank, Glacier, Montana, various county courthouses, Montana; FHL microfilm 1,902,880.

[154] "Winnett – Phillips, Vane," Great Falls Tribune (Great Falls, Montana) 19 Sep 1961, Page 5

[155] "United States Census, 1920," database with images, FamilySearch (https://familysearch.org/ark:/61903/1:1:M8QQ-8GL : accessed 28 December 2018), Pasku Popeska in household of Albert G Amundsen, Plentywood, Sheridan, Montana, United States; citing ED 204, sheet 6B, line 100, family 139, NARA microfilm publication T625 (Washington D.C.: National Archives and Records Administration, 1992), roll 975; FHL microfilm 1,820,975.

[156] "Treasure State Deaths," Great Falls Tribune (Great Falls, Montana) 25 Mar 1965, Page 26

[157] "Treasure State Deaths," Great Falls Tribune (Great Falls, Montana) 19 Mar 1973, Page 4

[158] "United States Census, 1940," database with images, FamilySearch (https://familysearch.org/ark:/61903/1:1:VBQH-Y53 : 15 March 2018), George Regis, Township 2 Ward, Ravalli, Montana, United States; citing enumeration district (ED) 41-6, sheet 13B, line 69, family 296, Sixteenth Census of the United States, 1940, NARA digital publication T627. Records of the Bureau of the Census, 1790 - 2007, RG 29. Washington, D.C.: National Archives and Records Administration, 2012, roll 2227; "United States Census, 1930," database with images, FamilySearch (https://familysearch.org/ark:/61903/1:1:XCMB-5ZK : accessed 27 December 2018), George Regis, Ward, Ravalli, Montana, United States; citing enumeration district (ED) ED 7, sheet 6A, line 44, family 141, NARA microfilm publication T626 (Washington D.C.: National Archives and Records Administration, 2002), roll 1260; FHL microfilm 2,340,995; https://www.findagrave.com/memorial/95705879; https://www.findagrave.com/memorial/85262945/bessie-regis; "Montana, County Marriages, 1865-1950," database with images, FamilySearch (https://familysearch.org/ark:/61903/1:1:F34S-5BJ : 11 March 2018), George K Regis and Genevieve Iten, 07 Oct 1950; citing Marriage, Hamilton, Ravalli, Montana, various county courthouses, Montana; FHL microfilm 1,905,839."Montana, County Marriages, 1865-1950," database with images, FamilySearch (https://familysearch.org/ark:/61903/1:1:F3Q1-QZG : 21 September 2017), George Regis and Bessie Jeanetta Wright, 19 Sep 1925; citing Marriage, Ravalli, , Montana, various county courthouses, Montana; FHL microfilm 1,905,837.

[159] "United States Census, 1940," database with images, FamilySearch (https://familysearch.org/ark:/61903/1:1:VB3Y-K6J : 15 March 2018), John Ristoff, School District 71 Sunday Creek, Custer, Montana, United States; citing enumeration district (ED) 9-31, sheet 1A, line 35, family 9, Sixteenth Census of the United States, 1940, NARA digital publication T627. Records of the Bureau of the Census, 1790 - 2007, RG 29. Washington, D.C.: National Archives and Records

Administration, 2012, roll 2216; "United States Census, 1930," database with images, FamilySearch (https://familysearch.org/ark:/61903/1:1:XCMJ-JPD : accessed 27 December 2018), John Ristoff, Miles, Custer, Montana, United States; citing enumeration district (ED) ED 4, sheet 9B, line 76, family 183, NARA microfilm publication T626 (Washington D.C.: National Archives and Records Administration, 2002), roll 1254; FHL microfilm 2,340,989; "Find A Grave Index," database, FamilySearch (https://familysearch.org/ark:/61903/1:1:QVLJ-VY26 : 13 December 2015), John Ristoff, 1967; Burial, Miles City, Custer, Montana, United States of America, Custer County Cemetery; citing record ID 95417469, Find a Grave, http://www.findagrave.com

https://www.findagrave.com/memorial/125037804/james-ristoff; "Montana, County Marriages, 1865-1950," database with images, FamilySearch (https://familysearch.org/ark:/61903/1:1:F37B-25Z : 21 September 2017), John Ristoff in entry for Alex Ristoff and Betty Indergard, 21 Nov 1948; citing Marriage, Sidney, Richland, Montana, county courthouses, Montana; FHL microfilm 1,905,317; "Find A Grave Index," database, FamilySearch (https://familysearch.org/ark:/61903/1:1:QV2P-8K88 : 13 December 2015), Florence Ristoff, 1930; Burial, Miles City, Custer, Montana, United States of America, Custer County Cemetery; citing record ID 79727812, Find a Grave, http://www.findagrave.com; "Ristoff Funeral Slated Monday," The Billings Gazette (Billings, Montana) 11 Aug 1963, Page 7; "John Ristoff," The Billings Gazette (Billings, Montana) 04 Sep 1967, Page 5; "Citizenship Hearing is Held in Miles City," The Billings Gazette (Billings, Montana) 15 Apr 1938, Page 13

[160] "United States Census, 1940," database with images, FamilySearch (https://familysearch.org/ark:/61903/1:1:VBQZ-SZG : 15 March 2018), Norman S Shotnokoff, Brockton, School District 55, Roosevelt, Montana, United States; citing enumeration district (ED) 43-28, sheet 1A, line 7, family 4, Sixteenth Census of the United States, 1940, NARA digital publication T627. Records of the Bureau of the Census, 1790 - 2007, RG 29. Washington, D.C.: National Archives and Records Administration, 2012, roll 2228.

[161] "United States Headstone Applications for U.S. Military Veterans, 1925-1949", database with images, FamilySearch (https://familysearch.org/ark:/61903/1:1:QV1Z-XT3R : 15 March 2018), Norman Shotnakoff, .

[162] "United States World War II Army Enlistment Records, 1938-1946," database, FamilySearch (https://familysearch.org/ark:/61903/1:1:K857-P8X : 5 December 2014), Norman Jr Shotnakoff, enlisted 26 Apr 1942, Missoula, Montana, United States; citing "Electronic Army Serial Number Merged File, ca. 1938-1946," database, The National Archives: Access to Archival Databases (AAD) (http://aad.archives.gov : National Archives and Records Administration, 2002); NARA NAID 1263923, National Archives at College Park, Maryland.

[163] "United States Social Security Death Index," database, FamilySearch (https://familysearch.org/ark:/61903/1:1:JT3K-DTY : 19 May 2014), Norman

Shotnakoff, Apr 1967; citing U.S. Social Security Administration, Death Master File, database (Alexandria, Virginia: National Technical Information Service, ongoing).

[164] "United States Census, 1920," database with images, FamilySearch (https://familysearch.org/ark:/61903/1:1:M8Q7-BNV : accessed 28 December 2018), Chris Sotir in household of William J Coffee, Butte Ward 3a, Silver Bow, Montana, United States; citing ED 207, sheet 8A, line 36, family 4, NARA microfilm publication T625 (Washington D.C.: National Archives and Records Administration, 1992), roll 976; FHL microfilm 1,820,976; "United States World War I Draft Registration Cards, 1917-1918," database with images, FamilySearch (https://familysearch.org/ark:/61903/1:1:K8QV-VZF : 13 March 2018), Christ Sotir, 1917-1918; citing Silver Bow County, Montana, United States, NARA microfilm publication M1509 (Washington D.C.: National Archives and Records Administration, n.d.); FHL microfilm 1,711,444; "Montana, Military Records, 1904-1918," database, FamilySearch (https://familysearch.org/ark:/61903/1:1:QP2Z-T4QH : 2 November 2018), Christ Sotir, 27 May 1918; citing Military Service, Butte, Silver Bow, Montana, United States, Montana State Historical Society, Helena. "Montana, County Births and Deaths, 1840-2004," database with images, FamilySearch (https://familysearch.org/ark:/61903/1:1:QKNR-DBFQ : 4 August 2017), Christ Sotir Sater, 26 Jul 1961; citing Death, Butte, Silver Bow, Montana, United States, various county recorder offices; FHL microfilm 2,312,130.

[165] "United States Census, 1920," database with images, FamilySearch (https://familysearch.org/ark:/61903/1:1:M83L-N4V : accessed 30 December 2018), Nick Spiroff, School District 122, Fergus, Montana, United States; citing ED 116, sheet 2A, line 8, family 29, NARA microfilm publication T625 (Washington D.C.: National Archives and Records Administration, 1992), roll 970; FHL microfilm 1,820,970.

[166] "Idaho, Southern Counties Obituaries, 1943-2013," database with images, FamilySearch (https://familysearch.org/ark:/61903/1:1:QLWX-TNGD : 8 November 2017), Louie Stonoff, ; citing Obituary, Pocatello, Bannock, Idaho, United States, Blackfoot Idaho Family History Center, Idaho; FHL microfilm 100,464,044; "Tudor Dimitroff Rites Monday," The Montana Standard (Butte, Montana) 02 Feb 1958, Page 28.

[167] "Find A Grave Index," database, FamilySearch (https://familysearch.org/ark:/61903/1:1:QVK8-H9HB : 13 December 2015), Louie Stonoff, 1980; Burial, Pocatello, Bannock, Idaho, United States of America, Mountain View Cemetery; citing record ID 43134816, Find a Grave, http://www.findagrave.com.

[168] "Asks $3,500 Damages for Alleged Assault," The Butte Miner (Butte, Montana) 28 May 1922, Page 6

[169] "Bulgarian Fight is Settled by Jurors," The Anaconda Standard (Anaconda, Montana) 25 Nov 1922, Page 6

[170] "Greeks Show Interest Trial of Assault Case," The Butte Miner (Butte, Montana) 17 May 1922, Page 11

[171] "Bulgarian Fight is Settled by Jurors," The Anaconda Standard (Anaconda, Montana) 25 Nov 1922, Page 6

[172] "Find for Plaintiff in Last Court Case," Ravalli Republic (Hamilton, Montana) 30 Jun 1950, Page 2; "Jury Term Ends in Ravalli County," The Missoulian (Missoula, Montana) 02 Jul 1950, Page 12

[173] "Seeks a Divorces," Fergus County Democrat (Lewistown, Montana) 25 Nov 1915, Page 7; "United States World War I Draft Registration Cards, 1917-1918," database with images, FamilySearch (https://familysearch.org/ark:/61903/1:1:K8QD-VNH : 13 March 2018), Christo Dimitre Tanaskoff, 1917-1918; citing Fergus County, Montana, United States, NARA microfilm publication M1509 (Washington D.C.: National Archives and Records Administration, n.d.); FHL microfilm 1,684,037.

"United States Census, 1930," database with images, FamilySearch (https://familysearch.org/ark:/61903/1:1:XCM5-67G : accessed 31 December 2018), Christo D Tanaskoff in household of Leonard O Jacobson, School District 13, Lewis and Clark, Montana, United States; citing enumeration district (ED) ED 27, sheet 1A, line 7, family 1, NARA microfilm publication T626 (Washington D.C.: National Archives and Records Administration, 2002), roll 1258; FHL microfilm 2,340,993; "News Notes," Great Falls Tribune (Great Falls, Montana) 07 Apr 1916, Page 3; "Discharged from Jail," Great Falls Tribune (Great Falls, Montana) 06 May 1925, Page 6; "1934 Auto Plate is Cause of Arrest," The Montana Standard (Butte, Montana) 30 Jun 1935, Page 20

[174] The Butte Miner (Butte, Montana) 01 Apr 1923, Page 2

[175] The Anaconda Standard (Anaconda, Montana) 26 Apr 1923, Page 3

[176] "District Court News," The Butte Miner (Butte, Montana) 27 Apr 1923, Page 7

[177] "Rankin Avers No Law to Hold Man," The Anaconda Standard (Anaconda, Montana) 20 Dec 1923, Page 2

[178] "30 Days Penalty for Petit Larceny," The Montana Standard (Butte, Montana) 03 Sep 1936, Page 5

[179] "United States Census, 1940," database with images, FamilySearch (https://familysearch.org/ark:/61903/1:1:VBQD-981 : 16 March 2018), Steve Tanaskoff in household of Elanor Paddock, Ward 3, Butte, Election Precinct 13, Silver Bow, Montana, United States; citing enumeration district (ED) 47-15, sheet 5A, line 35, family 17, Sixteenth Census of the United States, 1940, NARA digital publication T627. Records of the Bureau of the Census, 1790 - 2007, RG 29. Washington, D.C.: National Archives and Records Administration, 2012, roll 2230.

[180] "United States Census, 1930," database with images, FamilySearch (https://familysearch.org/ark:/61903/1:1:XCMR-VK3 : accessed 28 December 2018), Steve Tanoskaff, Ringling, Meagher, Montana, United States; citing enumeration district (ED) ED 17, sheet 4A, line 8, family 28, NARA microfilm

publication T626 (Washington D.C.: National Archives and Records Administration, 2002), roll 1259; FHL microfilm 2,340,994.

[181] "United States Census, 1930," database with images, FamilySearch (https://familysearch.org/ark:/61903/1:1:XC9Q-79D : accessed 28 December 2018), Chris Tarpo, Harlowton, Wheatland, Montana, United States; citing enumeration district (ED) ED 10, sheet 3A, line 5, family 51, NARA microfilm publication T626 (Washington D.C.: National Archives and Records Administration, 2002), roll 1263; FHL microfilm 2,340,998.

[182] "United States World War I Draft Registration Cards, 1917-1918," database with images, FamilySearch (https://familysearch.org/ark:/61903/1:1:K8QF-VFR : 13 March 2018), Nick G Thompson, 1917-1918; citing Chouteau County, Montana, United States, NARA microfilm publication M1509 (Washington D.C.: National Archives and Records Administration, n.d.); FHL microfilm 1,684,108; "United States Census, 1940," database with images, FamilySearch (https://familysearch.org/ark:/61903/1:1:VB3R-8M8 : 15 March 2018), Nick Thompson, Ward 2, Great Falls, School District 1 Great Falls, Cascade, Montana, United States; citing enumeration district (ED) 7-7, sheet 81B, line 67, family , Sixteenth Census of the United States, 1940, NARA digital publication T627. Records of the Bureau of the Census, 1790 - 2007, RG 29. Washington, D.C.: National Archives and Records Administration, 2012, roll 2214; "United States Census, 1920," database with images, FamilySearch (https://familysearch.org/ark:/61903/1:1:M8QH-P3Y : accessed 27 December 2018), Nick G Thompson, School District 21, Teton, Montana, United States; citing ED 211, sheet 6A, line 24, family 9, NARA microfilm publication T625 (Washington D.C.: National Archives and Records Administration, 1992), roll 977; FHL microfilm 1,820,977; "N.G. Thompson, 55, Dies Here," Great Falls Tribune (Great Falls, Montana) 07 Nov 1946, Page 6; "N. Thompson Funeral Rites are Sunday", Great Falls Tribune (Great Falls, Montana) 08 Nov 1946, Page 8; "Denton Man Rigs Up Movie Show on Truck," The Independent-Record (Helena, Montana) 13 Nov 1928, Page 7; "$15,000 Estate Left by N. G. Thompson," Great Falls Tribune (Great Falls, Montana) 10 Nov 1946, Page 11

[183] "United States Census, 1940," database with images, FamilySearch (https://familysearch.org/ark:/61903/1:1:VBQQ-FL1 : 15 March 2018), James Tricoff, School District 18 Fulton, Lewis and Clark, Montana, United States; citing enumeration district (ED) 25-32, sheet 1A, line 23, family 7, Sixteenth Census of the United States, 1940, NARA digital publication T627. Records of the Bureau of the Census, 1790 - 2007, RG 29. Washington, D.C.: National Archives and Records Administration, 2012, roll 2222; "United States World War I Draft Registration Cards, 1917-1918," database with images, FamilySearch (https://familysearch.org/ark:/61903/1:1:K8QX-JT8 : 13 March 2018), John Tricoff, 1917-1918; citing Butte City, Montana, United States, NARA microfilm publication M1509 (Washington D.C.: National Archives and Records Administration, n.d.); FHL microfilm 1,684,103.

[184] "United States World War I Draft Registration Cards, 1917-1918," database with images, FamilySearch (https://familysearch.org/ark:/61903/1:1:K8QX-JT8 : 13 March 2018), John Tricoff, 1917-1918; citing Butte City, Montana, United States, NARA microfilm publication M1509 (Washington D.C.: National Archives and Records Administration, n.d.); FHL microfilm 1,684,103.

[185] "Charged with Passing A Worthless Check," The Butte Miner (Butte, Montana) 05 Jan 1918, Page 7

[186] "Proceedings of Board of County Commissioners," The Montana Standard (Butte, Montana) 20 Apr 1938, Page 8

[187] "United States Census, 1940," database with images, FamilySearch (https://familysearch.org/ark:/61903/1:1:VBQQ-FL1 : 15 March 2018), James Tricoff, School District 18 Fulton, Lewis and Clark, Montana, United States; citing enumeration district (ED) 25-32, sheet 1A, line 23, family 7, Sixteenth Census of the United States, 1940, NARA digital publication T627. Records of the Bureau of the Census, 1790 - 2007, RG 29. Washington, D.C.: National Archives and Records Administration, 2012, roll 2222.

[188] "John Tricoff, 81, Dies in Dillon," The Montana Standard (Butte, Montana) 24 Oct 1975, Page 2

[189] https://www.findagrave.com/memorial/133560097.

[190] "United States Census, 1940," database with images, FamilySearch (https://familysearch.org/ark:/61903/1:1:VBQ8-TMZ : 16 March 2018), Mike Ulani in household of Cecile Lome, Ward 3, Butte, Election Precinct 13, Silver Bow, Montana, United States; citing enumeration district (ED) 47-15, sheet 2A, line 7, family 3, Sixteenth Census of the United States, 1940, NARA digital publication T627. Records of the Bureau of the Census, 1790 - 2007, RG 29. Washington, D.C.: National Archives and Records Administration, 2012, roll 2230; "Montana, County Births and Deaths, 1840-2004," database with images, FamilySearch (https://familysearch.org/ark:/61903/1:1:QKNR-DNLZ : 4 August 2017), Mike Ulani, 28 Nov 1956; citing Death, Butte, Silver Bow, Montana, United States, various county recorder offices; FHL microfilm 2,312,129; "Mike Ulani," The Montana Standard (Butte, Montana) 01 Dec 1956, Page 17 "United States Census, 1930," database with images, FamilySearch (https://familysearch.org/ark:/61903/1:1:XC9M-5DT : accessed 31 December 2018), Mike Ulane in household of John Melody, Butte, Silver Bow, Montana, United States; citing enumeration district (ED) ED 11, sheet 5B, line 85, family 31, NARA microfilm publication T626 (Washington D.C.: National Archives and Records Administration, 2002), roll 1262; FHL microfilm 2,340,997.

[191] "James P. Vasileff, 85," The Montana Standard (Butte, Montana) 07 May 1982, Page 2

[192] "Mrs. Mary Yankoff," Great Falls Tribune (Great Falls, Montana) 31 Mar 1951, Page 4; "United States Census, 1930," database with images, FamilySearch (https://familysearch.org/ark:/61903/1:1:XCMJ-NQY : accessed 29 December 2018), Theodore Wassel, Miles, Custer, Montana, United States; citing

enumeration district (ED) ED 5, sheet 8A, line 24, family 146, NARA microfilm publication T626 (Washington D.C.: National Archives and Records Administration, 2002), roll 1254; FHL microfilm 2,340,989.

Made in United States
Orlando, FL
06 March 2024

44480446R00071